UR UVP IS VALUELES... ...CE IS

THE BEST IS OVERRA... ...NG

OUT FORGET TIME MANAGEME... ...OU

GH QUESTIONS BENEFITS DON'T SELL

IG FICTION DON'T LET TECHNOLOGY

EMENT YOU DON'T WANT CUSTOMERS

PERTISE IS A LIABILITY NOBODY NEEDS

UELESS PERSISTENCE IS IRRITATING

ST IS OVERRATED STOP ASKING SO

UT FORGET TIME MANAGEMENT YOU

GH QUESTIONS BENEFITS DON'T SELL

IG FICTION DON'T LET TECHNOLOGY

EMENT YOU DON'T WANT CUSTOMERS

PERTISE IS A LIABILITY NOBODY NEEDS

UELESS PERSISTENCE IS IRRITATING

S OVERRATED STOP ASKING SO MANY

GET TIME MANAGEMENT YOU DON'T

STIONS BENEFITS DON'T SELL BUYERS

Price is a cop-out

**FORGET
TIME MANAGEMENT**

YOU DON'T WANT CUSTOMERS

*Don't let technology
dumb you down*

BENEFITS DON'T SELL

BUYERS ARE IMPERFECT

Uncommon
SENSE

JILL HARRINGTON

Shift YOUR THINKING

Uncommon
SENSE

TAKE New Action

BOOST YOUR SALES

Figure.1
Vancouver / Berkeley

Cataloguing data is available from Library and Archives Canada
ISBN 978-1-77327-009-8 (hbk.)
ISBN 978-1-77327-010-4 (ebook)
ISBN 978-1-77327-011-1 (pdf)

Design by Jessica Sullivan
Illustrations by Lynne Morinan
Author photograph by Carmela Sagula

Editing by Karen Milner
Copy editing by Eva van Emden
Proofreading by Renate Preuss
Indexing by Stephen Ullstrom

Printed and bound in Canada by Friesens
Distributed in the U.S. by Publishers Group West

Figure 1 Publishing Inc.
Vancouver BC Canada
www.figure1publishing.com

Contents

Start here

I WROTE THIS BOOK with a single purpose: to challenge you to turn the traditional seller mind-set on its head. By eliminating the nonsense common in today's sales environment and replacing it with uncommon sense, you'll stand out and win better deals at higher prices.

I opened my business in 2002—an idiotic time to do this. The dot-com bubble had burst and 9/11 had shaken the planet. The world was in turmoil. But I was on a mission. I had worked with, led, and mentored salespeople for over two decades. And I noticed talented salespeople and business owners slam into a wall of frustration daily as the rapid advances of technology changed the way people communicate, do business, and buy. The world of sales was shifting, but they weren't.

Fast-forward to 2017. Now there's no shortage of books, webinars, blogs, infographics, videos, and websites to guide you through the individual steps of the sales process, to explain the intricacies of a complex sale, or demystify the world of social selling. But something is missing. Because, despite all of this sage advice, I continue to hear the same questions from sellers across industries and geographies:

- How do I stand out when my competitor claims the exact same benefits?
- How do I get in front of new buyers faster?
- How do I make the prospecting process more comfortable for me? And for the buyer?
- How do I loosen the stranglehold of an established supplier?
- How do I convert more leads into sales?
- How do I make the sale without dropping my price?
- How do I get the important stuff done with only twenty-four hours in a day?

How is it possible that these questions remain unanswered?

For starters, most sales advice focuses on "what" sellers should do. This has created a profession of "doers," many of whom are really smart people running around doing extraordinarily dumb things. And pressure from the boss to make more calls, get more meetings, and close more sales only adds to the insanity. Others are simply stuck in a rut. Doing what they've always done. Doing what the competition does. Mistaking the side of that rut for the horizon.

This book forces salespeople out of the rut. It requires you to think ... and to think differently about the problems you want to solve once and for all. It provides the "why": why these challenges persist, why specific approaches don't make sense, and why others do. And the "how": how to work smarter to move the sales process forward in a world where buyers are faced with a tsunami of sellers vying for their attention.

On the one hand, salespeople, we've never had it so good. We have a growing smorgasbord of social channels through which we are able to locate, connect with, and learn about desirable prospects. We have technologies that help us capture, organize, and leverage customer data to grow existing accounts and engage new ones.

On the other hand, buyers have become increasingly distrustful of sellers. E-mails and pitches claiming to grow revenues, reduce costs, or improve productivity are viewed as spam or seen as yet another slick marketing ploy with no real substance to back it up.

If your prospects are happy with the status quo, they have multiple ways to avoid interacting with you. And when it's time for a buyer to engage with a seller, she's already performed her own due diligence and, right or wrong, has formed an impression of you, your company, and your offering long before you talk.

Selling isn't rocket science. It is common sense. The problem with common sense is that it's regularly missing in action, and doing dumb things costs you time, energy, and business. The net results are slower sales cycles, profit-crushing negotiations, and lost deals, all of which hit your company's bottom line—and your own.

This book delivers counterintuitive thinking that highlights the idiocy of "Always Be Closing" and offers up a new set of selling ABCs that lead to bigger, faster sales. It eliminates sales clichés such as "elevator pitches," "unique value," and "closing techniques" from the smart salesperson's vocabulary. It will remind you that, despite the rampant advances of technology and social media, buying decisions are made by human beings. And human beings are icky gooey unpredictable individuals with their own unique perspectives.

This book will catapult you into the realization that finding the answers to all of your big hairy sales challenges requires you to shift the way you think. Every section shines a light on the common nonsense causing salespeople to unwittingly exacerbate their biggest challenges. And each delivers the uncommon sense and practical behaviors necessary to drive the sale forward.

This book is not intended to replace or compete with all of the extraordinary books written on the subject of selling.

It is my intent that those books will become more valuable to you after reading *Uncommon Sense*. The goal of this book is to stimulate thought and provoke change. It does not focus on the complex sale, the sales process, or the sales conversation. Where other books focus on "to do," this book focuses on "undo." You'll want to keep it front and center on your desk, tablet, or car seat as a personal go-to coach that will reset your thinking as you prepare for that challenging call, first client meeting, or important presentation.

The fundamental truth is this: Your results are driven by your actions. Your actions are driven by how you think. When you change how you think, you change your results— it's all uncommon sense.

For confidentiality and privacy, I have changed the names of some of the salespeople featured in the following chapters.

Get results from this book

WE LIVE IN A WORLD of sound bites. We have the attention span of a gnat. We want smart thinking, but we want it fast. Make it simple, make it relevant, and make it actionable. And above all, make it deliver tangible results. So I wrote this book for gnats. Each bite-size chapter is written in your language and supported with stories of the good, the bad, and the downright ugly: real salespeople, eye-opening statistics, and career-changing successes.

Here are five tips to make sure you get results from reading this book:

RESET
Read chapter 1 first to reset your thinking. Read with a curious mind—curiosity about your perspective, about your sales approach, about your actions. You won't agree with everything, but I'm OK with that. I just ask that you think deeply about the implications of the words on the page before reading further. Then move on to the other chapters, which take this new thinking through each step of the sales process, and finish in chapter 8, which will get you thinking about how to manage your #1 sales asset: you.

DIP

I suggest you read the book once cover to cover and then dip back into relevant chapters as needed. Struggling with your prospecting activity? Jump back to chapters 2 and 3 to clarify your purpose. Overwhelmed with everything on your plate? Dive into chapter 8 to manage your attention. Writing an important proposal? Revisit chapter 5 before you pitch to lose. And if you need to get grounded? Circle back to chapter 1 for a heaping dose of uncommon sense.

COMMIT

Think about your sales activity. Choose what from this book will most benefit you, and *commit to execute*. Don't try to do everything or you'll end up doing nothing. Create a new habit. Once you've mastered one element of uncommon sense, move to the next.

ENGAGE

Shared commitments have a higher likelihood of happening, so involve your peers. Have everyone on your team read the book. Use your team meetings to discuss a chosen tip in the context of your real world. Set a monthly team challenge. And commit to sharing your success stories at a future meeting.

REVISIT

Today many books are out of date by the time you say "Amazon." I wrote this book to be timeless. The uncommon sense in this book will outlive your career. So don't toss it on a shelf or let it hibernate in a drawer. Think of it as your personal coach when you need one. A self-help book for sales superstardom. Revisit the pages of this book over and over again, so that, for you, uncommon sense becomes common practice.

Enjoy the read.

MAKE THE SHIFT

Rethink Your Way to Sales Success

AFTER TWO DECADES of success, Leanne's business was tanking. A seasoned sales professional, she had built her business on a reputation for unparalleled expertise and quality work. But her persuasive telephone conversations highlighting the value of working with a premium provider were falling on deaf ears. Economic conditions had driven her best clients into the arms of cheaper competitors, potential new buyers weren't responding, and profits were nonexistent. Leanne had started to lay off staff, and when she called me, she was desperate. "Jill, I have left numerous messages, sent e-mails, and tried connecting via LinkedIn. And not one response. I can really help these companies. Why is no one interested in talking to me?"

Leanne was waist-deep in the mud-filled rut of habit. Her focus on being the best, getting the meeting, and closing the sale was killing her business. Compounding the problem, she was handing down this stale approach to her young sales team. All of this was leading the company to the brink of bankruptcy.

In a world where every seller claims to be the best, offer the highest quality of service, and deliver astronomical business results, why do sellers expect buyers to respond to hollow promises? And, as the internet provides buyers with access to a tsunami of information on just about every product, company, and person, why do so many sellers continue to see themselves as information providers?

No one needs your information. We are neck-deep in information overwhelm. I google the words "sales training, Toronto," and within one second I receive over five million results. So why would anyone want to receive information from me about sales training?

Face the facts.

In the eyes of our prospects, we all look and sound the same. You think it's hard to differentiate your offering? Buyers find it equally difficult to discern relevant differences between suppliers.

Behind every e-mail, RFP, meeting request, and buying decision sits a human being, and usually more than one. There are over seven billion human beings on this planet, which means over seven billion different perspectives. Each buyer's perspective is their individual reality. They don't view the benefits of what you sell the way that you do.

So if you rely on the features and benefits of your product, service, or brand to stand out in the eyes of your customers, you are simply training your customers to tune you out. You end up sounding and acting like everybody else. If you're convinced that getting the best proposal in front of me will wow me into your camp, then get ready to fall into the black hole of no deal. If you believe that your logical sales arguments will convince me to buy, think again. I'm not you!

Take the example of the financial services rep who is convinced the cost-saving benefit of his credit card service is reason enough for any business owner to buy. Every time I say "No thanks," he responds with different shades of the same closing questions: "Do you want to save money?" "Does your current service save you money?" "Have you thought about what it may be costing you not to look at alternatives?" Questions that make the customer feel like an idiot or the seller sound like one. Neither is good.

Consider the disappointment of the technology sales rep who, excited to discover his prospect has a problem that his company is uniquely positioned to solve, jumps straight to the offer of a proposal... Only to be blindsided by a competitor who took the time to explore the implications of the customer's need, finds a bigger underlying issue, and outsells his peer to win a deal worth ten times the original estimate.

And let's not forget the online consultant who assumed that because I chose to participate in one of his company's free webinars, I was ready to buy. After three failed attempts to get a response to his self-centered e-mails, he put the final nail in his coffin by implying I must be a moron for not wanting to "double my revenue" with the support of his service.

I think we all agree that it is time to put the old sales mantra "Always Be Closing" behind the gates of Jurassic Park along with every other sales dinosaur. "But hold on, Jill," I hear you say, "We are paid to close sales." Yes, you are. Salespeople are measured by and compensated for delivering results. Frankly, it's the profession where "no results" ultimately equals "no job." But here's the uncommon sense: *the sale is simply the output.* If you want to drive more sales at higher profits and with greater ease, you need to *focus on the right input.* The input is the thought process that drives the right behaviors and actions—depending on who the buyer is, and where she is on her individual journey—to move the sales process forward efficiently and appropriately for both buyer and seller.

Smart sales organizations recognize that one of the biggest opportunities to differentiate in today's world is through their sales approach: how they act, and interact, with their customers and potential customers. But here's a startling statistic. While 78 percent of vendors believe they differentiate themselves effectively through their sales approach, only 25 percent of customers agree.[1] This suggests that more than half of you operate under the impression that your sales conversations and interactions help you stand out in the eyes of the customer. And they don't! Enter the most dangerous blind spot in selling today.

Salespeople are smart. So how is this possible? Here's my observation. Like Leanne, many of you are stuck in a rut doing what you've always done, doing what your competitors do, or simply doing what worked in the past. But it doesn't work today. It's simply common nonsense.

The good news is that this represents a big opportunity for those of you who are willing to rethink selling. Let your competition continue to compound their ineffectiveness while you commit to your position in the elite tier that gets noticed. You'll read numerous examples of how to do this throughout this book. But the right input starts by shifting how you think about selling.

Stop striving to be the best

ADRIANA, A PROFESSIONAL BUYER for a large manufacturing company, shared five competitive responses she had received to her RFP (request for proposal). Each contained a variation of the common sales claim, "We have the most experienced team in the industry." She laughed at the absurdity: "Sure, everyone is the best!" But she was deadly serious when she said, "How do we make a decision when we have to wade through this marketing fluff?"

Of course you're the best in class. You beat the competition in every respect: attention to detail, customer care, quality, and value. Unfortunately, so does everyone else.

Let's face it: "Being the best" does *not* guarantee the win. Take Nicky's situation. Nicky enthusiastically shared with me the status of a bid for a new client that would translate into a multiyear contract and millions in revenue. "The final step of the process is the client's visit to our office for a full presentation. We're pulling out all the stops. Signage in the lobby. A red carpet greeting by the staff. Our president is kicking off the presentation. We've written the best proposal. It's beautifully bound. No one else in the industry can touch us. We've got this one, Jill. It's in the bag!"

Only it wasn't. Two weeks later the client called Nicky to tell her they awarded their business to a competitor. We've all been there. Convinced that your product or service offers the perfect fit for Client X, you make your pitch, stage a sharp presentation, and ask for the order, only to see X select an inferior competitor. "What an idiot. He'll regret this decision," you mutter. "Can't he see we're the best?"

Sales pros are obsessed with being the best. And, in a world where the best has become meaningless, buyers are sharing a consistent message: "When three proposals look almost the same, which they frequently do, we'll award the business to the second- or third-best if that will save us money and help us get faster approval to move forward." Translation: Customers worry more about making a good decision than making the best decision.

Partnered with this craving to be the best is the ludicrous addiction to finding your "uniqueness." The Unique Value Proposition is like the Holy Grail of selling, and searching for it has sent sales organizations on lifelong quests. Frankly, most company value propositions aren't particularly unique. And when I ask salespeople, even their leaders, to articulate a tight, clear Unique Value Proposition, most can't.

Even if you are remarkable enough to identify authentic uniqueness, it's inevitably short lived. Before you have time to spell "unique," an astute competitor will replicate it and, on the heels of your success, do it better and cheaper.

Don't confuse marketing with selling. While claiming to be the best and pitching your unique value may work as slick marketing to the masses, they are ineffective sales tools. While it's easy to fill your messages, proposals, and presentations with hot air, it takes effort to articulate why, and how, you are right for this particular customer and her situation.

The bottom line is this: Sellers need to spend less time seeking a Unique Value Proposition, and more time developing Value Propositions *Unique to each client*.

UVP > VPU

So if all these unsubstantiated claims of being the best make your prospect grimace, how do you replace the frown with a nod of approval? The simple answer: You get relevant.

Get relevant

MAUREEN, THE TRAINING MANAGER for a national media company, was referred to me. Her company currently works with two other training organizations. She was interested in speaking with me because "we have a very seasoned sales force, Jill, but our training has become stale. We need some fresh thinking to refocus and reenergize the team." After a short phone conversation about her organization's business environment, her sales team, and how they were hoping to reverse a downward trend, Maureen suggested I come in to meet with three of her directors. "Jill, come prepared to share some information on salesSHIFT and how you're different than our current training partners."

Already I felt like I was heading into a no-win meeting where I would sound and behave like every other sales trainer on the planet. I offered an alternative. "Given the situation you just shared, I'd like to suggest an alternative approach. Rather than provide a comparison to your current providers, how about I use my hour to demonstrate how salesSHIFT may be more relevant to achieving your company's end goals?"

She loved it. "Which means," I continued, "I need a little more information from you. And your directors will want to come prepared to share their perspectives on the situation and their aspirations for the team."

The ensuing meeting sizzled. The directors had the floor for the first forty minutes and spoke passionately about their vision for the sales organization and their view of the existing challenges. I sat back and listened. Then I used their words and the remaining twenty minutes to talk about salesSHIFT in the context of their objectives. In short, I was able to say less with considerably more credibility. And with far greater impact. I made no reference to the existing training partners. They were irrelevant. We all walked away excited to take the next step together.

The question I get asked most by sellers is, "How do I differentiate my company from my competitors?"

My response: "What do your customers care about most?" They care about themselves, their company, and their success. Their own interests and priorities. Fact: Attention, time, and money flow to priorities. And I mean priorities by the customer's definition, not yours.

Buyers crave relevance. And they're not getting it because although sellers are busy providing information about *their* company, service, or solution, they fail to *position* the right attributes *in the context* of what matters most to the specific buyer. In short, they fail to make it relevant to the customer.

Relevance doesn't just apply to your offering. It applies to the sales messages you create and the proposals you present. Relevance is critical to achieving a return on your investment from your trade show presence and networking events. Relevance dictates the productivity of your client meetings.

Of course it's important for you to understand who you compete against. But a focus on trying to be different from, or better than, the competition is ineffective and exhausting. If you want to stand out, it's not that complicated. Shift your energy from being the best to being the most relevant.

How do you do that? Execute the new triad of selling ABCS.

Rewrite your selling ABCs

I RECENTLY POSED this question to a conference audience: "What do you see as the biggest challenge in selling today?" A hand in the front row shot up. "The level of skepticism about salespeople!" declared Graham. It wasn't the answer I had expected, but it's right on the money. Statistics show that distrust of the sales profession has tripled in the last ten years and continues to climb.

This is a problem, because trust is the bedrock of sales success. As a prospective buyer, I may be happy to take advantage of your expertise, squander your valuable resources, and get a comparative quote. Thank you. But without a high degree of trust, I will *not* buy from you.

Trust is not something to which we are entitled because we send out a creative e-mail, host a free webinar, or spew a list of obvious benefits. It can't be earned through the declaration of some cheesy line, "I'm not here to sell you something. I'm here to partner with you." Nobody believes that junk.

Earning trust starts with your intent.

Most sellers have the same intent: Find a need and close the sale. Always Be Closing. But this no longer works—for buyer or seller. Establishing a buyer's trust requires shifting your intent. This brings me to the #1 ABC in selling today:

Always Be Contributing

Every prospecting message, every call, presentation, proposal, and meeting must contribute value. Simply put:

Trust is earned by contributing relevant value over time. If you're not contributing value, you are simply adding cost, wasting time, and making yourself indistinguishable.

Unfortunately, "value" is one of the most overused and abused words in today's business vocabulary. It's a term peppered through every sales communication with little thought given to its meaning. Take Midori, the vice president of a third-party agency (the middleman), who saw her company being cut out of the buying process. Revenues had plateaued as a result of long-standing clients choosing to work directly with manufacturers. "They no longer see the value in our services," she said. Her plan to resolve the issue was to sequester her entire executive team in a boardroom and thrash out ideas to rearticulate the company's value. My question to her, "How many customers and prospective customers will be at the table?" was received with silence.

Who defines value? The receiver. Not the giver. In order to be relevant, you must contribute value by *the buyer's* definition, not yours. And this requires you to execute the second of the new selling ABCs.

Always Be Curious

I met Peter in one of my training classes. An advertising sales veteran, Peter had worked with many of his customers for almost two decades and had strong professional and personal relationships with them. His sales results reflected this. He was candid when he introduced himself on day one of training: "Jill, I'm not sure what you can teach me, but I'm open to listening." At the end of day two, Peter left the class with a new appreciation for the meaning of curiosity and the inspiration to take action.

Three months later I received his enthusiastic call. "Jill, I'm on track to make target this month." Peter was not referring to his monthly quota. He was talking about hitting his annual goal. In July!

He attributed his success to entering his client meetings with an open mind. His customers were used to him showing up armed with a traditional set of questions and his recommendations for their upcoming media campaign, but a new Peter was on their doorstep. A supersized Peter who flexed his new-found curiosity muscle and unearthed clues to new opportunities simply by being interested in his client's perspective. The result: an immediate 300 percent increase in revenue.

"Jill, we assume we know our customers and what makes them tick. We don't." Peter was right. On top of that, he discovered that human beings appreciate others who are genuinely curious about their world. This approach is a key distinction from the traditional information gathering by sellers with a single intent to close a deal.

So let me be clear on my definition of curiosity. Curiosity is not the act of asking a bunch of questions to get the information to make the sale. If you've been on the receiving end of one of these mind-numbing fact-finding interrogations, you'll understand why buyers scurry for cover behind e-mail and the RFP process. Every seller is trained to ask questions to discover needs. This is important, but it's not enough. And it's not curiosity.

Curiosity is a genuine interest in people and business. Curiosity is neither manipulative nor packed with hidden agendas. Curiosity is hearing something and wanting to learn more, observing and wanting to understand why, reading and wanting to go deeper. Curiosity is a catalyst for your learning and growth as a human being and as a business professional. It delivers insights that enable you to communicate with prospects in ways that are meaningful to them, and that are welcomed, not ignored.

In my previous role as a corporate executive, I spoke about "selling" at industry conferences around the globe. As a key decision influencer within my company, I had no shortage of vendors vying for my attention at breaks and lunches. Many who wanted to introduce themselves turned out to be afflicted by a violent case of verbal diarrhea about their product and company, mercifully healed when I accepted a business card. Those cards went into my left-hand pocket. Some approached me to discuss the topic presented or to obtain a different perspective on something shared, while others wanted to talk about the implications of the current market or get to know me and my organization. These cards went into my right-hand pocket. The right-hand cargo returned to the office with me. The left didn't. Fact: In a world where everyone strives to be "interesting," people who are genuinely interested stand out.

Curiosity should not be packed away, like the best china, waiting for that important client meeting. Curiosity should start before your first attempt to connect and continue through the entire sales cycle and beyond to ensure lasting relationships and future business growth.

Curiosity may kill cats, but it is essential to the survival of today's professional seller. My advice to sales leaders seeking high-potential candidates for their organization, "Use the interview process to test candidates' genuine curiosity about business and people. It is hard to teach, yet fundamental to your ability to out-sell your competitors." I'll share specifics on how to apply this ABC to get faster access to good prospects, unearth bigger opportunities, and oust cheaper competitors in the following chapters.

So the right kind of information is power, right? Well, no. Selling power comes from having quality information and, more importantly, how you use this information to position your offering to be the most relevant to this specific customer. This brings me to the third of the new selling ABCs.

Always Be Connecting

Some of you will remember life before the internet. Before the advent of the web, e-mail, social media, and CRM systems, it was a different world. If you wanted data on a prospect or client, you called to request a corporate brochure and thought nothing of waiting a week for it to land on your desk. Finding potential prospects required a drive to the local library to plow through a doorstop of a business directory that was already out of date by the time it hit the shelf. Similarly, buyers seeking information about available products and services had no choice but to pick up the phone to talk with a sales rep or request a brochure. Anyone under forty is laughing at the absurdity of this. Even I struggle to imagine how we functioned. Those days are long gone.

Technology has forever shifted the way people and companies buy, and how and when they choose to interact with salespeople. The internet has fast-forwarded us through the information age into the quagmire of information overwhelm, leaving buyers bloated with information and paralyzed by choice. The last thing they need from a sales rep is more information. They can visit your company's website, Facebook page, blog, YouTube channel, and myriad other online and offline resources to get all the information they need.

So why are so many sales messages, proposals, e-mails, and presentations nothing more than a series of information dumps? And how can you possibly expect this approach to engage a customer already drowning in a tidal wave of marketing?

Today's buyers choose to research potential purchases without supplier involvement. They neither need nor want your information. Instead they expect you to bring three things to every interaction:

1. An understanding of the customer's world.
2. Relevant expertise.
3. The ability to connect the two.

Simply put, the buyer's mind-set is: I need you to *connect* your information to me and my world in ways that contribute to my success, as I define it. Otherwise good luck getting my attention. And my business.

We assume buyers make the connection between our offering and their companies' needs. They don't. That's our job. We presume that our promises of saving money, increasing revenue, or driving more leads to their business will have every buyer salivating. They don't. Your ability to stand out in the fog of information has nothing to do with your features, benefits, expertise, or brand. It has everything to do with how you position these attributes in the context of what's important *to the buyer*. Make the shift from pitching to positioning. Put your information in the context of what matters most from your customer's perspective. I'll be sharing a number of real client examples of how this concept of positioning applies to your prospecting messages, your presentations and proposals, and a heck of a lot more throughout this book. For now, tattoo these three pieces of the selling puzzle on your brain:

While these simple ABCs may be common sense, they are not easy to execute. One of the biggest barriers to applying them is the very thing our customers seek from us: our expertise. Expertise is an extremely valuable asset. But it is commonly accompanied by the ugly stepsister that drives so much common nonsense: assumption.

Experts assume that the customer makes the connection between their offering and his needs. As a result they fail to demonstrate why they are the most relevant choice to the customer. Experts assume they know what is best for their clients. As a result they neglect to get curious. Expertise can lead us to articulate what *we* believe to be of high value to any specific customer, rather than what actually is most important to that person. To shift away from this presumption, to eliminate the common nonsense, and to master the new selling ABCs, the first step is to kick off your shoes.

Kick off your shoes

AT A RECENT CONFERENCE I asked for a volunteer with a size eight and a half foot to come to the stage. Preferably a woman. Paula came up. We stood side by side facing the audience. I asked Paula if she would be willing to wear my shoes. Literally. She said yes. She stepped out of her fairly sensible low-heeled pumps while I sat on a chair to unstrap the six buckles of my narrow-fitting suede heels. We exchanged shoes. After a couple of attempts to step into my shoes, Paula asked if she could use my chair. While I continued to talk to the audience, Paula struggled with the finicky straps but eventually stood up.

"How was that?" I asked.

"Difficult," she replied. "Your feet are obviously way narrower than mine, Jill. And how do you deal with these things every day? There's so much fussing. These tiny buckles are demonic!"

"OK. And how do you feel now that they're on?"

"Bloody uncomfortable! How do you walk?"

What was the point of this exercise? Paula's huffing and puffing demonstrated how tough it can be to step into another person's shoes. Particularly when the other person's skinny feet and taste for high heels are the polar opposite of her own.

And what was the first thing Paula did to make it possible to wear my fab footwear? She had to step out of her own. Every day salespeople with a size eight wide foot unconsciously attempt to step into their customer's size seven narrow shoes without first kicking off their own, usually with disastrous outcomes.

Linda was about to lose her best customer, a multi-million-dollar account. Market conditions had forced her largest account to look at cutbacks in a number of areas across the company. The high-ticket employee incentive programs designed and executed by Linda's company were not exempt. Todd, the marketing director, had been asked by his executive team to explore lower-cost providers and had advised Linda to make adjustments to her traditional recommendations and sharpen her pencil this year.

Linda was confident. She had a strong relationship with Todd, and her company had a successful track record with his executives. She was well acquainted with the expectations of their employees. They appreciated quality, high levels of creativity, and the support of an experienced team. She knew what was right for this account. And she knew her competitor. Their lower price reflected a lack of experience and resources to manage the caliber of program her client expected. Linda cared about the success of her client. She was acting in his best interest when she loaded her proposal with inclusions she knew were critical to delivering a triumphant program for Todd. She was convinced she could convey the importance of paying her higher rate.

The following week Todd called with disappointing news. Linda missed the mark. The decision was final. He was awarding the business to her competitor. The breakup was painful. Linda was shocked, but she shouldn't have been; she made a fatal mistake.

Linda was an expert on her company's services. She knew her client. But she neglected to get curious about the changed circumstances, and she failed to connect her offering to the new priorities. As a result, her client didn't see her contributing the most relevant value. And no relationship could save that. She lost a lucrative three-year contract to a less experienced supplier because she made important decisions about the sale while standing in her own shoes.

Stepping out of your shoes and into your customer's is extraordinarily hard to do when you are under pressure to close deals or achieve monthly quotas, or when the survival of your business is at stake. It's even harder when, as in Linda's case, the customer's perspective is incongruent with your own. Salespeople fall into the trap of creating messages, asking questions, and submitting proposals based on what they believe *should* be important to the customer rather than what actually *is*. This professional pandemic of "shoulding" all over the people that matter most to our success is frustrating both sellers and buyers.

Sarah is a classic example. The sales manager for a large downtown convention center, she is fortunate to have a steady stream of incoming leads from conference organizers. So why is she discouraged? "Many of these callers are shopping around and comparing our venue to less expensive facilities. It's ludicrous. I've tried to educate them. They should realize that being centrally located in a facility with state-of-the-art technology and an impeccable array of services will attract more exhibitors and attendees. They should see our higher rates as a solid investment, not a cost. I guess I need to do a better job of convincing them."

Sarah has a bad case of the "Shoulds." Preaching the benefits in an effort to "educate" customers and prospects is not the remedy to her big hairy sales challenge. Or yours. Sarah first needs to kick off her shoes. Exercising her curiosity to fully understand her customers' situations will help her choose one of the two potential forks in the road. One path will lead her to the realization that there is not enough reason, from the buyer's point of view, to buy from Sarah. The second provides her the valuable information that will

allow her to connect relevant benefits to the buyer's interests. Ultimately, pricing becomes a secondary issue.

Sarah prides herself on being customer focused, as does
her company. Its website, and her presentations and sales
messages, are choking with declarations of commitment to
the customers' interests. "Our customers are our #1 priority." "We pride ourselves on our customer focus." "The customer comes first."

But here's the uncommon sense that begs you to step out
of your seller's shoes:

Are you focused on your customer from the *customer's*
perspective?

Or, like Linda and Sarah, from a seller's perspective?

This question leads us to the importance of your "pause
button."

Hit the pause button

JASMINE IS AN ACCOUNT EXECUTIVE with a destination management company (DMC) in the US. Her company handles all of the ground services for many of the large corporate groups and conferences coming to her city. Evening events, parties, team building activities, plus logistical arrangements like transportation, entertainment, and décor are all part of the mix.

When one of the convention hotels in the area passed on a lead, Jasmine was cautiously excited. An international corporation was bringing a large group to the hotel later in the year. It was the first time that the event would be held in this city, and the client, Phil, planned to use the services of a knowledgeable destination management company. He had selected a vendor, but contracts hadn't been signed, and he was open to having a phone call with others in the area who had been recommended by the hotel sales manager.

Knowing that Phil already had a preferred vendor, Jasmine was unsure how to approach the call. Her colleagues had provided some guidance: "Talk about our relationship with the hotel. Provide examples of what we've done there. Talk about our creativity and expertise. Share our history and reputation with this destination."

As she shared with me her plan to wow Phil with her company's impressive credentials, she sounded unconvinced. I was too. Every other DMC in the city was going to do and say the exact same thing. Not only would this approach commoditize Jasmine's service, it would do little to establish trust. And it was unlikely to engage a stranger whose greatest fear was "yet another seller trying to convince me her company is better than my original choice."

"Jasmine," I suggested, "let's hit the pause button. Let's step out of our shoes into Phil's for a moment and think about this call from his perspective. What do we know about him?" Together we hashed out what we knew and where we had some gaps that Jasmine could fill with a little curiosity and research.

Stepping back and pausing to see the situation from the client's point of view rather than simply forging ahead to close the sale in the usual way brought Jasmine to two important conclusions. First, Phil was responsible for the single most important event run by his company, and he was bringing it to a destination he was not familiar with. That constituted risk. Finding the right DMC would minimize his risk, and was likely the reason he was entertaining calls from multiple destination experts. Second, this was only one of many events that this organization hosted across the country. So in addition to the immediate sale for Jasmine, this call represented an opportunity to build a foundation for future business for one or more of her affiliate offices in other cities.

This call was not simply about a sale. It was about differentiating Jasmine and her company from the competitors by taking a more thoughtful approach to the conversation. How she opened the call, either from a mind-set of closing or from one of contributing, would dictate whether or not Phil would fully engage.

Jasmine paused to approach this opportunity intentionally and with the customer's goals in mind, not just her own. She kicked off her shoes and stepped into Phil's. She decided to open the call with empathy for this buyer's situation and a clear articulation of her intent. "Phil, I understand that this is your first time coming to our city, and finding the right

DMC is essential to your confidence in the success of this program. I also recognize that you have choices. So my goal for this call is to help you get to the right decision for your group. Of course I'd be thrilled to have you choose my company. But let's see if that makes sense from your perspective. Why don't we start with you sharing a little about your group and what's important to you as the person responsible? Then I can share a little about our services in the context of your specific interests. By the end of the call, we'll both have the information we need to decide if there's value in taking the next step. How does that sound?"

Of course she was still prepared to share benefits of working with her DMC. But she was able to hold back and position only those that were relevant to this specific client, at the right time in the conversation. Her approach was not only a differentiator in helping to advance this sale, it also laid a foundation for trust, ensuring that this buyer would put out the welcome mat for Jasmine's company in future years.

By giving herself permission to pause and think deeply about the call from both parties' perspective, Jasmine made this call matter.

Once in a lifetime!

EVERY SALES BOOK talks about the importance of preparation. Unfortunately, many salespeople believe that time to prepare is an unaffordable luxury. As a result, relying on intuition, better known as "winging it," often trumps forethought. Even those of you who do take the time to prepare may be doing so with an unconscious and lopsided bias toward your own perspective as the seller.

The senior VP of sales for a large technology company recently joined his team of sales managers in training because he wanted to deepen his understanding of their methodology. On the final day, he shared his epiphany with the group: "It occurs to me that while we do a phenomenal job of preparing for our client meetings from our point of view, we do little to prepare from the customer's perspective. Frankly, I'm not even sure that we fully understand their expectations because we're not asking up front. We are diluting the productivity of our meetings and calls. This has to change."

Now think about this.

> Every interaction with a customer,
> potential customer, or prospect
> is a "once in a lifetime moment of truth."

You will never again be with this specific individual or group of buyers, under these circumstances, at this point in time. Never.

Once in a lifetime!

The sales process—how you acquire new business, grow existing relationships, hang on to your best clients in the face of fierce competition—is nothing more than a series of these individual once-in-a-lifetime interactions.

And every moment of truth—whether it's a phone call, e-mail, tweet, meeting, presentation, networking event, or tradeshow—is your opportunity to deliver one of three possible outcomes:

1. **A positive impact.**
2. **A negative impact.**
3. **No impact.**

I mean impact on the customer's perception of you, and impact on the progression of this sale, and possibly future sales. So doesn't it make sense to make every interaction matter?

Making it matter takes thought—uninterrupted, focused time to think, which is something many of you believe the busyness of your role in this fast-paced, time-starved world will not accommodate. Who has time to think? Plus, the dogged pursuit of shortcuts, the reliance on the crutch of technology, and the quest for "easy" have resulted in the sales profession becoming so systematized, templated, and scripted that we are unconsciously creating a culture of non-thinkers. The evidence is in the unproductive prospecting scripts, canned presentations, and cookie-cutter proposals that position many salespeople just one notch above telemarketers. Thoughtful preparation is not simply "nice to do." It is an *essential step* in the sales process that will help you assure your differentiation and ultimately accelerate your progression through the sales cycle.

Make the shift

SO YOU GET THIS. Success in sales is not just about what you do. It starts with how you think. Extraordinary sales professionals think deeply about their clients when preparing their calls, presentations, and proposals. This mind-set influences how they act. Making the shift from fixating on the output (closing the sale) to focusing on the input (the triad of new ABCs) is the first step to driving stronger sales results. Contribute to your customers' success by being guided by their definition of value, not yours. And, once and for all, dump the common nonsense.

Common Nonsense		Uncommon Sense
Strive to be the best	→	Get relevant
Always Be Closing	→	Always Be Contributing
I know	→	Always Be Curious
Provide information	→	Always Be Connecting
Unique Value Proposition	→	Value Proposition Unique to each client
Seller perspective	→	Customer perspective
It's a sales call	→	It's a once-in-a-lifetime opportunity

So now to the important stuff. How do you convert this uncommon sense thinking into new action at each step of the sales process so that you are *always* perceived as a contributor of relevant value? So that you stand out in a crowded landscape? So that you boost your results with bigger, better sales?

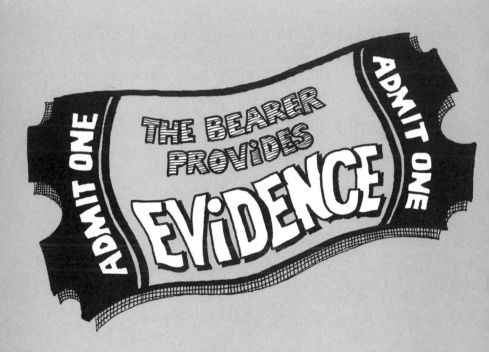

ACCESS

Get in Front

of Good Prospects

Faster

AS JOHN WALKS UP to the turnstile, he's excited about the ball game. "Ticket!" barks the gate attendant.

"I don't have a ticket," replies John confidently. "But let me share the benefits of allowing me access. I'm small, so I don't take up much space. I'm a big fan and will cheer louder than anyone else. I'll buy a hot dog, which means I am boosting revenue. And I always dispose of my trash, so my seat will be left tidy."

"Son, you need a ticket to get into the game. Go back to the office and buy one." John leaves and the following day walks up to the same turnstile.

"Ticket!"

"I don't have a ticket," says John. "But let me share the benefits of allowing me access."

"No ticket, no access!"

To enter the game you need a ticket. Common sense, right?

And yet every day salespeople approach their prospective customers' turnstiles with nothing more than a well-worn script and a tired list of benefits, expecting to be granted access.

And when they fail, just like John, they show up again and again because "persistence pays."

Right?

Wrong.

Today's buyer is faced with an assault of unsolicited sales messages. Sellers hit them via the phone, e-mail, and myriad social channels with one intent: to plow their way through the prospect's fortified door to make a sale.

I PICK UP THE PHONE. Eric is at the other end. Charismatic and funny, Eric shares that his company can shoot me to the top of the search engine rankings and drive business to my site. My response, "I don't have time right now. Is there somewhere I can read a little more about your service?" Translation: Like the vast majority of prospects today, I prefer to do my due diligence without overbearing pressure from a stranger paid to sell. Eric's warm tone turns downright frosty. He pushes me to continue the conversation. I won't be pressed. The call comes to an abrupt end.

Sure, it's an OK strategy for paid lead generators and telemarketers who continue to play the torturous numbers game, throwing mud at an infinite number of walls and hoping something will stick. But it's not a smart approach for sellers looking to develop profitable long-term business relationships.

It used to be that closing was the toughest step in the sales process. Today the greatest challenge is opening: gaining access to an initial productive conversation. And it's the step in the sales process that makes even smart sales pros slide back to the "nonsense" end of the common sense scale.

Just think about a typical unsolicited sales message from the busy buyer's perspective:

Based on a thirty-second voice mail or e-mail, you're expecting me to voluntarily give up thirty minutes of my precious time to talk, meet, or do coffee with a stranger. During this time you will talk interminably about the "unique" benefits of working with your company and then endeavor to sell me something I don't want. Or try to convince me that you are better than my current spectacular supplier, to whom I would gladly donate my left kidney.

Why would I agree to do this? I barely have time to talk to the people I need.

And when the first approach fails, the follow-up campaign involves more of the same until, after three frustrating attempts to reel in a live one, most sellers give up.

So what's your ticket to the game of prospecting?

Your ticket to access = Evidence

The reality is, I don't want to hear from you unless you provide evidence that you have something of value that will contribute to my success in areas that are important to me now. Evidence that you have something that will contribute to my success starts the process of establishing trust. Without it, no amount of persistence will convince me to open the door to you or give you another minute of my time. If I don't trust your motives, any attempt to gain access will be inefficient, or worse, brings the sales process screeching to a halt.

Developing personalized messages that demonstrate this evidence takes effort. If you're not prepared to invest energy into identifying something specific about me, my company, or my market so that your prospecting messages address my current interests, guess what—you're heading to the prospecting black hole along with every other seller who decided it's easier to talk about his product than to talk about the customer.

Providing evidence is not pulling some factoid from my website and quoting it at the front of your message. This simply proves that you can read. Evidence in prospecting is acknowledging something that you know is important to me and then demonstrating your relevance by explicitly *connecting* your value to that priority.

An example of the common nonsense that hits my voice mail: "Mrs. Harrington, I'd like to talk about your banking needs. Please give me a call back at your earliest convenience."

Contrast this with someone using uncommon sense by providing evidence and making the connection: "Mrs. Harrington, we know that protecting and growing hard-earned profits are top priorities for small-business owners. Our small-business team works exclusively with busy owners like you to eliminate unnecessary fees, protect capital, and help you make smart investment decisions so that your returns grow faster."

If you can't make a relevant connection between my interests and your offering, you're not providing evidence, you're providing spam.

You want faster access to good prospects? Invest in a ticket. How do you do that? It starts with your mind-set—how you think about prospecting.

Your prospecting
mind-set matters

I MET MARCI at a marketing conference for entrepreneurs. She was fiercely proud of the service her accounting firm provided to mid-size businesses. She knew that she brought immense value to her market. But every time she picked up the phone or fired off an e-mail to a new prospect, she felt like she was pimping her worth. And while she had adopted a less intrusive approach by beefing up her social media presence, the results were far from inspiring.

Corporate sales reps are no different. For many, prospecting activity is a necessary evil that inspires the same level of enthusiasm as a root canal. Many follow the traditional "wash, spin, and rinse cycle." Spell out your company's awesome value proposition in an e-mail. Replicate to multiple names on your list. Connect with likely looking suspects on LinkedIn. Attempt a couple of follow-up phone calls. Repeat. Business development activity for the week: Check! You're taking action. Just one problem: You're not seeing results. And this takes a toll. I've seen very capable salespeople, worn down from beating their heads against the brick wall of "no response," leave their jobs entirely.

When I ask salespeople what they consider to be their biggest barriers to gaining access, most point to issues outside of their control. RFPs, voice mail, gatekeepers, the competitor's stranglehold relationship. The internet is crawling with advice, good and bad, on what to do to overcome these barriers. The reality is these external roadblocks pale in comparison to the internal roadblock you throw into your own path. The real antagonist in your prospecting story is your mind-set.

The way you think about prospecting shapes your actions, which in turn dictate whether you hit frustration or pay dirt. Many of you are reluctant prospectors. And this reluctance is driven more by the fantasy swirling inside your head than by what's happening in your market. For example:

Common nonsense: The purpose of prospecting is to bull-doze your way through a heavily barricaded door.

This belief is firmly tied to the old-school mantra of "Always Be Closing." It's why Marci felt like the class nerd asking the prom king for a date every time she picked up the phone. "This is such an uncomfortable call. He's not inter-ested in me. He'll say no." This attitude leads you to create the kinds of hollow or irritating messages that disengage the very people you are trying to attract.

Given that today's buyers choose to do much of their early research, sourcing, and shortlisting without the inter-ference of a paid sales professional, it's time to rethink your purpose.

Consider that the real purpose of prospecting is:

> To be favorably positioned
> on the right prospect's radar.
> Before he is ready to engage.

Or, better still, to accelerate his interest in speaking with you before your competitors.

Bottom line: You want the right prospects thinking of you first when the time is right for them.

Common nonsense: If you deliver a great message, you'll get a response.

Wishful thinking! Your compelling and relevant message increases your odds of getting on my radar. But it won't guarantee a response, at least not immediately. Every day is the right day for you to sell something. It isn't always the right day for me to buy. Lack of response today is not synonymous with lack of interest tomorrow. I may intend to get back to you. But guess what gets in the way? Busy does. Priorities do. That unanticipated fire burning within my company. Prospecting is not an event. Don't expect me to remember you because you sent one or two great messages. Take responsibility for being remembered. Prospecting is a process.

Be prepared to invest in the prospecting process.

Common nonsense: Persistence is good.

If prospecting is a process, surely that requires persistence. Fifty seven percent of customers say that persistence helps them keep a potential vendor on their radar screen.[1] I believe that number would be considerably higher if we focused more on *how* we persist rather than just persisting. A weekly onslaught of "I'm checking in," "Just following up," or "I haven't heard back from you" is more irritant than persistent.

How you persist secures a response.

Mind-set matters. Replace the common nonsense about prospecting with these fundamental truths:

1. Your purpose is to be #1 on my radar.
2. Prospecting is a process requiring you to contribute relevant value over time.
3. *How you persist secures a response.*

Now before you apply this revised thinking, your first step is to know who you plan to access so that you go after the right ticket. The one that gets you access to the VIP line.

Stop kissing frogs

ADAM HAD SIX HUNDRED names on his prospect list. A shortage of leads was not his problem: Managing them was. Firing out templated sales messages was delivering weak results. Frustrated and overwhelmed, Adam asked, "What is the best way to stay in touch with a list of over six hundred prospect accounts?"

"Sorry Adam, I don't have an answer." It's a crazy question. There is no way to communicate effectively with a list of six hundred. The more enabling question is, "How do I take a smarter approach to organizing and prioritizing my prospect accounts so that I am in touch regularly with the ones that matter most?"

The answer: Separate the princes from the frogs.

Whoever said "You have to kiss a lot of frogs to find a prince" got it wrong. I say, "Go straight for the prince!" Sure, prospecting is a numbers game. Without consistent activity you're not going to access new buyers. But choose to play a smarter game, and you have a greater chance of accessing the best, most profitable prospects.

No matter the size of your list, this is the universal truth:

Not all prospects are equal.

So don't treat them as such. You can attack your list one name at a time—an arduous, uninspiring slog. Or you can choose the smart approach and separate your princes from your frogs. Your princes are the VIPS (very important prospects) on your list. Those you have defined as most winnable and most desirable. Prioritize your attention and actions so that you invest thought and effort on the princes who will lead you to the kingdom of riches.

To begin, first define them, then find them.

Define your VIPs by answering these five questions:

1. **What are the common characteristics of your best customers?** Those for whom you do your best work. The ones you most enjoy working with. Who are the most profitable. Get curious and leverage this knowledge to find more of the same.

2. **Why have companies sought out your services or products in the past?** Look at the events, issues, and problems that triggered the interest of your existing customers. Who else faces these same issues?

3. **What is your organization's advantage and who will most benefit from it?** This is the distinct promise (and it's likely you have more than one) your company brings to the market. At salesSHIFT our advantage is our focus on training sales pros to *think* before they act. I look for industries that are stuck in a selling rut. And within those industries, for companies that are eager to climb out. And I seek companies hiring fresh young sellers who want to get it right straight out of the gate.

4. **What is your personal advantage?** And who would most benefit from this? I am referring to the specific attributes that you personally bring to your potential clients. Pierre transitioned from a legal career to his current role as a technology sales rep. His deep understanding of the interests and specific nuances of the legal profession enables him to quickly establish credibility with legal firms. Hence they are on his VIP list.

5. **Who do you have easy access to at the appropriate level of influence?** Which of your prospects are directly connected to

people you know? Your contacts can give you access to valuable information about the prospects on your list—information that can help you craft compelling messages. Better still, they can provide a credible introduction.

Once you've created a profile of your VIPs, get out there and proactively find them. Use these criteria in four ways to accelerate the process of getting in front of the *right* prospects:

1. **Identify the VIPs within your current list.** These are always the priority. Be deliberate and thoughtful and follow the new ABCs when creating your messages and preparing for meetings with these contacts.

2. **Proactively seek out more VIPs.** How do they find new suppliers? Look for where your princes hang out online and elsewhere. Be where they are. Listen and learn. Contribute relevant value. Initiate the process of getting on their radar.

3. **Share your VIP profile with people in a position to refer you.** Give me the data that makes it easy for me to flip through my mental and physical database of contacts so that I can introduce you to people and organizations that you want to reach. And that want you.

4. **Filter incoming leads and referrals through your VIP criteria.** Have a handful of qualifying questions at your fingertips to quickly separate the princes from the frogs. You'll find help with this in the next section.

Apply every stitch of the uncommon sense in this book to your VIPs.

And what do you do with the frogs? Once you've taken care of the princes, expediency rules. You can pull out that templated e-mail or dial for dollars with your best script. And, when it makes sense, delete. After all, who really wants to kiss a frog?

Caution: Incoming frogs

YOU CAN CHOOSE to be strategic about your prospecting, actively seeking out the princes rather than aimlessly smooching a bunch of frogs. But sometimes those frogs leap into your net uninvited.

For example, I was booked by one of the US State Tourism Authorities to speak to its members at an annual conference. At the time, the tourism authority was required to share all incoming leads with its hotel members. This created a problem. A client, specifically seeking a four-star waterfront hotel for a big event, also received responses from optimistic three-star city-center hotels. It was an exercise in futility for some of the sellers and frustration for the buyer.

Who doesn't love a steady flow of buyers landing in their inbox? It's the ultimate goal of our social activity and marketing efforts. And sales pros are programmed to react to opportunity. Any opportunity. "I might be able to convince this company that city center is preferable to waterfront." Incoming is easier. It's more comfortable. It's immediate. Proactively generating your own leads and meetings takes effort.

But there are a couple of serious problems with incoming leads.

Think of the implication of this statistic: 74 percent of today's B2B buyers conduct more than half of their research online before making a purchase.[2] Translation: By the time that lead hits your inbox, they know far more about you than you do about them. They have options, and you are already up against stiff competition—and likely heading toward a price war.

Plus, you have little control over who drops into your inbox. You may end up kissing a lot of frogs. And that usually means spending time on marginal opportunities that suck your attention away from proactively seeking your princes.

Now I am certainly not saying that incoming leads are bad. I love them as much as the next person. But not all leads are equal, and one seller's prince may be another seller's frog. So here's a litmus test to tell the frogs from your princes, to sort the duds from your VIPs. It's a handful of "qualifiers," questions that will quickly identify if, and how much of, your attention should be invested in any given lead.

Your qualifiers will be specific to your company and market, designed to obtain vital clues to the winnability and desirability of the opportunity. These questions will help you assess the account while also efficiently establishing your credibility with the caller. I have five qualifiers that I use when I receive an incoming request for sales training. Each is chosen with very specific intent.

1. **Why is this a priority for you/your organization? And why now?**
   This big-picture, open-ended question centers on the customer. In addition to seeking to understand their situation, I'm listening for clues to a compelling or strategic business reason for this purchase. If this issue is an organizational priority, then there will more than likely be available funding to move it forward.

2. **What needs to happen (or change) in order to accomplish this?**
   As a subset of the first question, I dig a little deeper into the issue and their objectives. I'm now listening for the buyer's perspective on how they plan to address their challenge. This gives me something tangible to which I can connect my services and opens the door for me to offer an expert

perspective or, potentially, an alternate viewpoint that provokes thought and deepens my credibility.

3. **What is the process for ensuring you make the right decision? And where are you in the process?**
I want to know who I am speaking to, who I should be speaking to, and how the decision will be made. The second part of the question not only gives me an opening to ask about the competitive situation, it also gives me a clue about how winnable this customer is for me. For example, if I'm being brought in at the tail end of the process, that's a red flag that requires further exploration.

4. **How will you know that you have found the right provider?**
In addition to having the buyer think about and articulate a response to this query, the question provides clarity on whether I am a viable contender. I recently chose to walk away from a referred opportunity because my company's focus and expertise didn't match the type of support this buyer was looking for. Not only did I feel that I wouldn't win, I didn't want to win.

5. **How are you funding this initiative?**
I avoid or defer asking "What is your budget?" because it immediately focuses the customer on a fixed number and derails the conversation. We do eventually talk numbers, but my initial interest is in identifying if they have adequate funding. If not, are they motivated to obtain it? If they do provide a number, I will ask, "How did you come to that specific figure?" The answer to that one is gold dust.

Leads that come our way without much effort always look attractive on the surface. But face it—a frog is a frog. Define your own qualifiers to avoid the temptation to chase frogs. Then focus your attention on the best use of your valuable time, your VIPs. Even if this requires you to go searching for them.

Evidence is TOP of mind

MY PHONE RINGS. I don't recognize the number but nevertheless choose to pick up. I'm ready for a sales call. A confident voice at the other end says: "Good morning, Jill, this is David at Company Y. We help businesses like yours grow faster by providing you a constant stream of pre-qualified leads. Does that sound of interest to you?"

I'll bite. "Damn right it does, David. How do you do that?"

"We interview you to identify your target audience and then create messages that our team uses to contact potential prospects on your behalf. We qualify them and provide you the best leads."

"So you're a lead generation company. David, you said you help businesses like mine. What do you know about my company?"

Silence.

Maybe he didn't hear me. "David, do you know what we do at salesSHIFT?"

"Well, Jill, I planned to take a look at your site. Just ran out of time. But I will take a look when I get off this call."

"Not good enough, David. Call me back when you've done some homework. Let me know how, and why, you think you can provide specific value to me."

"OK, I'll do that. Thanks, Jill."

A month later... the phone rings. I pick up.

"Good morning, Jill, this is David at Company Y, and we can help you grow your business faster by providing you a

40

constant stream of pre-qualified leads. Does that sound of interest to you?"

I'm gobsmacked. David is back. "David, hello! Good for you. So what did you learn about me?"

Click. And David was gone.

In a world where there is no shortage of information about any person, company, or industry, we know that attempting to connect with a VIP without doing basic research is like jumping out of a plane without a parachute. Insane. But hovering at the plane door analyzing wind speed and cloud coverage and double-checking your pack won't get you to the ground.

Beware the affliction that cripples prospecting efficiency: paralysis by analysis. It's a condition that can creep up on you and eat hungry chunks out of your valuable selling time if you don't manage it appropriately. Hit the right balance. Step into your prospect's shoes. Focus your research on uncovering what's TOP of mind to her, and use this as evidence to which you can connect your value.

T: Trends and Threats. Look for trends and threats within your prospect's industry, market, or company to which you can contribute value. A trend may be a shift in consumer buying habits. A threat may loom as a new breed of competition is about to disrupt your prospect's market.

O: Objectives and Opportunities. Organizations publish their vision, mission, and goals all over the web: websites, social profiles, blog posts, videos. There is no shortage of places to look. If company X is looking to be the market leader by 2018 and you see an opportunity to accelerate their progress through your offering, you've found evidence of value you can contribute. A reason to connect.

P: Priorities and Problems. Look for evidence of both current and future strategic priorities and the associated problems that may hinder forward movement. If you have evidence to suggest you can accelerate the process or minimize a barrier, you're in a position to print your ticket.

The more specific your TOP of mind understanding, the better. If it relates directly to the company (they are looking to improve employee retention by 20 percent in the face of new higher-paying competition) or the person (John has been charged with hiring sixty new telesales professionals in the next twelve months) and you have definitive ways to help, you've hit the bull's-eye.

Often more readily available, but not quite as powerful evidence, TOP of mind understanding can also relate to an industry (new regulatory controls threaten to hinder how industry XYZ conducts business) or a role (meeting planners are seeking a stronger voice at their company's executive table). The point is, if you want access to new buyers, you need a ticket or you'll be waiting in a very long line. A valid ticket is evidence that you understand what's TOP of mind to this buyer and, more importantly, that you have something of *relevant* value to contribute.

Accessibility to information means that doing your homework before you seek access to prospects is a baseline expectation for anyone outside of the telemarketing ranks. The depth of your research will relate to the desirability and winnability of any given prospect. You know this. And yet, despite investing in this important step, many sales messages never hit the prospect's radar. Why? Failure to leverage the evidence you worked so hard to uncover.

Why your messages fail

BEN, A SEASONED sales professional, was in the black hole. After months of leaving voice mails and firing out e-mails, he was no closer to getting a meeting with John, the CEO of a Los Angeles-based company. He wanted this client. It would reap hundreds of thousands of dollars, potentially millions long term, in revenue for his company. He just needed a few minutes with John. Why had his carefully crafted e-mails and phone calls resulted in silence?

Ben was hitting the wall of silence because he was focused on the output rather than the input.

1. **His messages were designed to "get a meeting."** They were having the opposite effect.

2. **His e-mails were loaded with powerful benefits "unique" to his service and company.** They were white noise to the customer, who had heard the exact same thing from others.

3. **Ben was persistent.** But his persistence was nothing more than a series of repetitive e-mails and voice mails aimed at . . . well, you know . . . getting in the door.

Ben was looking for a surefire technique when he solicited my help.

"Let's cut the BS," I told Ben. "Buyers are numb to this impersonal jabber. Consider the situation from the CEO's point of view. Give him evidence that his time will be well served if he responds to you. Here's a framework that will help you position the evidence John needs to grant you access. Go out and make it happen."

Three days later I heard from Ben. His meeting with the CEO was scheduled, his flight to LA was booked, and he had a whole new sense of clarity about what it takes to succeed in prospecting.

I didn't give Ben a bulletproof script. I provided a framework. Because I wanted Ben to think—think about John. Scripts are easy. Frameworks are efficient.

Every day, salespeople let profitable opportunities slip by them because they choose easy over efficient.

So you made twelve calls today and fired out forty e-mails this month: Congratulations! You hit your call target. No question, activity is critical to sales success. But the push to make more calls and see more clients is downright dangerous when this activity isn't balanced with the right actions. Impotent voice mails and valueless e-mails that masquerade as sales activity fail to move the VIP buyer relationship forward and result in nothing more than client apathy or irritation.

Why is it that so many salespeople spend a crazy amount of time preparing for a presentation or crafting a winning proposal, but fire out prospecting messages like they are handing out Girl Guide cookies? Face it, you won't be writing many proposals or making any presentations if you can't get in front of new buyers. So here's the Let's-Cut-the-BS framework I provided Ben. The one that gained him immediate access to his high-profile VIP.

L: Lead with the customer's interests.

C: Connect your value.

B: Be specific.

S: Say less with more impact.

When I receive an unsolicited e-mail, voice mail, or other form of communication from a seller, I want to hear evidence in the form of two important facts:

- That you know something about me. And I mean something that's important (TOP of mind) to me by my definition, not yours.
- That you have something of specific and relevant value to help resolve this issue that is important to me.

Failure to provide evidence of these two points leads me to the conclusion that somehow my name got on your list. You know nothing about me, and so I see no benefit in talking—and you'll undoubtedly waste precious minutes of my day trying to convince me to buy something I neither want nor need. How badly do I want that?

Delete. Clearly not the response you are looking for.

WHY DO MOST prospecting messages fail? Because most sellers believe that benefits sell. Sellers lead with *their* perception of value, not the customer's.

For example: "Hi, Alan, this is Jill with salesSHIFT. We help sales organizations drive higher revenues and profits in less time. I'd like to talk to you about how we might support the success of your sales organization. Please give me a call at 905 . . ."

What sales leader doesn't want higher revenues and profits? They all do. So what's wrong with this message? The buyer can't hear it! All they hear is "blah blah and more blah." I've missed the most important step. I failed to get Alan's attention by first talking about Alan.

Lead with the customer's interests:

Messaging is counterintuitive, which is why it mostly misses the mark. Too many sellers lead with what they have to sell, gushing an endless stream of generic benefits. But what do customers care about most? Themselves, their success, their issues. So here's the uncommon sense:

> You get the buyer's attention when
> you talk about him. Not about you.

Consider how differently Alan would perceive my message if I focused on his interests: "Alan, ... Jill with sales-SHIFT. I recently read about your strategy to grow your sales organization: Hire fresh young brains out of college. I am sure, like every sales executive, your priority is to get this new team driving results. Fast.

"We train sales pros to *think* differently so they act efficiently. Straight out of the gate. We've seen some remarkable revenue results with millennials. Worth a fifteen-minute introductory call to hear about your situation and share some of these results?"

See the difference?

Connect your value:

A prospect hears your value only when it's connected to something important to him. That's how you *seal his interest.*

I did my homework in advance of the call so that I could lead with the prospect's situation. I know from experience that efficiently bringing newbie sales reps up to speed so that they quickly contribute revenue is TOP of mind for sales leaders. Yes, I talked about the benefits my company can offer, but I connected them to what's relevant to Alan. Advancing his strategy by accelerating the ramp up of his new hires. I provided evidence that I have something of specific and relevant value to a priority issue by Alan's definition. Evidence that suggests it's a worthwhile investment of his time to give me a ticket to a first conversation.

Be specific:

Because specifics sell!

I shared specific value. I can help him shift the way his sellers *think*. And we've had good results with *millennials* (the majority of new recruits on his sales team). Even more important, I shared what I plan to do with this valuable fifteen minutes of Alan's time: "Better understand your situation and, more importantly, share some of the success we've achieved with others in the exact same situation." Not only am I leveraging the evidence I worked so hard to uncover, but Alan also now knows specifically what he's going to get from a next step, which minimizes his *perceived risk* of engaging with me.

Say less with more impact:

A prospect has the attention span of a gnat. Need I say more?

As I did in the example above, say all you need to say in less than forty-five seconds on a voice mail or one paragraph in an e-mail.

All of this is common sense. Right? But unfortunately LCBS is uncommonly executed.

If you are one of the many sellers who chooses to skip the L (Lead with the customer's interests) in the LCBS framework and instead lead with "my company's great benefits," you are sabotaging any chance of being noticed.

So why do so many intelligent sales professionals put their success in jeopardy? Because they prefer to worship at the altar of "easy." And it's a heck of a lot easier to talk about you than to talk specifics about a new prospect. But easy doesn't work in selling. It takes thought and effort to lead with what is TOP of mind to the customer. If you choose easy over efficient, or if you believe that selling requires no effort, here's some tough love: Get out of sales!

And here's a gentler kick in the pants. Put down this book. Take a look at your own prospecting messages. Do they follow the LCBS framework? Have you uncovered and articulated the evidence that enables you to lead with the customer's interests? Have you directly connected specific relevant value? And have you created a concise, relevant message to provide meaningful impact? I've lost count of the number of sellers who, like Ben, were struggling to engage a VIP in a first conversation, but who got the green light after making this one thoughtful shift to LCBS. Now that's selling efficiency.

Never say this!

YOU NOW HAVE the uncommon sense LCBS framework for positioning your messages so that you stand out. Please don't nullify the impact by incorporating any of these seemingly innocuous statements that regularly show up in sellers' e-mails, disengage the customer, and guarantee your place in the deleted mail folder.

Never say this!

1. **"I'd like to get five minutes of your time."**
   Liar, liar pants on fire! We all know that this is a classic "bait and switch" technique. You know you want, and plan to take, more of my cherished time. I don't know of any human being with an IQ over ten who buys this line.

   I like that you include a time parameter for your call. Just be honest. And minimize the risk by letting me know specifically how you plan to use my time. It will encourage me to respond. Assuming you've shared relevant value in your e-mail, you might say something like, "Jill, I'd like to schedule an introductory twenty-minute call to get your perspective on the above and to share results we've achieved with other professional services firms." OK, now it sounds doable, believable, and a good use of my precious twenty minutes.

2. **"Our greatest differentiation is our dedication to long-term relationships and our attention to detail."** And from a different seller: **"What sets us apart: Team of seasoned professionals. Attention to detail. Smooth operations. Financial stability."**
   Seriously! There's not even a whiff of differentiation in these unoriginal claims. They do nothing to set you apart. What's

more, every one of them is a baseline expectation. It's like trying to attract the right mate on a dating site by saying, "I am upright and breathing. What more do you want?"

Recall my example of the sales message to Alan in the "Why your messages fail" section. I didn't talk vaguely about increasing revenue. I talked about the specific way in which we boost the efficiency of a new team of millennials so that they drive higher revenues—because I know Alan is hiring a new team of millennials. Give the reader something specific that shows you have thought about him. That's a differentiator.

3. "We work with companies like yours."

I have no problem with this statement if your message includes some indication that you actually know what my organization does. But I see a proliferation of e-mails making this claim with nothing to substantiate it. Frankly, I don't believe you. And, in the unlikely event I do respond, you'd better be ready to answer two questions: "What similar companies have you done work for? And what results did you achieve?"

4. "We have proven expertise."

Says who? You? You're paid to say this! If you have proven expertise, show me the evidence. Quote the source that corroborates this statement. Did you win an award? Do you have examples that authenticate your claim? Have you included a client testimonial that provides proof of your impact on their organization?

5. "I look forward to hearing from you."

This, or some variation of the same, seems to be the favorite sign-off line in e-mails and voice mails. It's a lovely sentiment. But you know that the odds of hearing from me are one step below a lottery win. And here's the bigger concern. You've just given up control of the sales process. Always close your message (regardless of delivery method) with a clear articulation of your next step. Here's an example of a better closing statement for a first e-mail: "John, I'll follow up with a call on Thursday. If you wish to connect before then, I may be reached at..." This tells your prospect three important facts: You are serious about connecting. You are not going away. You would welcome a response.

6. **"I am following up from the e-mail I sent over last week. Are you available for a call to discuss how the inclusion of self-directed learning driven by an integrated career-pathing agent can elevate the learning function beyond the cyclical nature of performance-driven development plans?"**

"Huh?" This kind of pompous jargon leaves me speechless. This impenetrable e-mail went to an organizational development executive, a man who understands learning systems and career paths without the need for a translator. But this had him stumped. Hoping to impress by loading your e-mails with confusing verbiage and unimpressive "corporate speak" will not further your cause. Use simple concrete language that will get you noticed for the right reasons.

Using any of these hackneyed lines in your sales messages suggests that you expect a buyer to be impressed with stuff that takes you all of sixty seconds to concoct or cut and paste. Now that's just nonsense.

Stop calling high

IF THERE'S ONE PLACE you definitely need a valid ticket to gain access to, it's the C-suite. Without it you have less than a microscopic hope of entry to this level of customer.

Simon wanted help preparing a message that would help him access the CIO within one of his accounts. I asked him to share a little about the CIO. His information was sketchy. There was absolutely no evidence to suggest the CIO would derive any value from speaking with Simon. So I asked why he wanted to meet with this CIO. "We've been told by the boss to call high because that's where decisions are made."

Worst advice ever! For Simon. Simon had six months of business experience under his belt. He had no experience speaking with anyone at the executive level. Not even his own senior team. And he'd be hard pressed to distinguish between gross margin and EBITDA. Calling high would have been a suicide mission.

Simon is not alone. In a study that asked executives for their perspective on seller preparedness for an executive meeting, only 22 percent felt that sellers "can relate to my role and responsibilities within the organization." A mere 24 percent felt that salespeople "are knowledgeable about my specific business." And this next one scares me most because it points to the lack of critical evidence and questions the salesperson's reason for being there: Just 22 percent of these executives believed that sellers "understand my issues and where they can help."[3] The old adage "Start high, because it's easier to get shuffled down the ranks than up the decision-making hierarchy" is only smart if you are equipped to call high. And if it makes sense.

Now I'm not saying *never* call high. I am saying don't blindly aim for the top because someone told you it is the right thing to do. Your access strategy depends on a number of factors:

1. Your offering.

One of my most successful clients admits she never calls at the executive level because "I have no illusions about our service. It's a tactical service that is of no interest to the CEO."

2. Your level of business acumen.

Are you capable of holding a conversation at this level? Are you genuinely interested in business strategy, and do you have evidence that connects your service to advancing the strategic priorities of this company?

3. The buying process and preferences of the company.

Francis, the CIO of a large technology company, does not respond directly to sales calls and e-mails. "I have a team that I respect and empower to put the right people in front of me as appropriate." Given Francis talks only to sellers recommended by these trusted influencers, you may be spinning your wheels trying to enter the process high while your competitor is being walked in by a more friendly contact lower down the chain.

If you want to reach prospects at the senior level but aren't confident in your ability, adopt a strategy of like-level calling. Get your own executive involved at the top while you're nurturing relationships in other areas of the company.

Of course aiming for the top can be the right way to go. The key is that your messaging must be appropriate to the role and interests of the person you send it to. Do your homework. Don't make assumptions. For example, do not assume that a middle manager is not a strategic thinker. Check out your prospect's LinkedIn profile; look at how they write about themselves and their company. Know who you're talking to.

In addition, to be adequately armed to make an approach at this level, I recommend tapping into information sources and coaches on top of doing your own research. A source is someone who may have little to no influence but who is a non-threatening supplier of relevant information. They know the company, the issues, and the culture. In my case these are salespeople within the company or industry. The information I have obtained from these chatty sources has enabled me to create messages that land me on their bosses' radars.

I seek the support of coaches from inside and outside the prospect company. These are smart people who know first-hand the trends, market forces, and executive issues in the industry or company I am seeking to enter. One of my best coaches for the hospitality industry is an executive and for-mer client. I meet with him regularly to top up my under-standing and get the perspective of an influential executive within this industry.

And most importantly, if you plan to call high, take per-sonal responsibility for developing your business acumen. Learn about business through your conversations with your customers. Talk to your own senior team. Read business books, and listen to executives online. And take courses. One of the most valuable courses of my sales career was "Finance for Non-Financial Managers," a program I took on my own dime. It gave me a whole new appreciation for how executives make decisions. It introduced me to their lan-guage. And enabled me to better connect and articulate my value to an important echelon of buyers.

Make the shift

YOU WANT ACCESS? You need a ticket. Without a mind-set of curiosity, it's impossible to uncover the TOP of mind evidence that will get you noticed. Crafting messages that pique interest requires you to hit the pause button and stand in the receiver's shoes before attempting to connect your value to his or her need. Start with the right mind-set: "How can I contribute to this prospect's success?"

Then work smart. Define the right organizations (your VIPs) and prioritize your attention accordingly. Identify the right people (the appropriate level of customer). And grab their attention by ruthlessly applying the LCBS framework to demonstrate you have evidence of value by their definition.

Common Nonsense		Uncommon Sense
Benefits open doors	→	Evidence accelerates access
Prospecting is an event	→	Prospecting is a process
Plow through the door	→	Position to be #1 on your prospect's radar
Treat all prospects equally	→	Prioritize your VIPs
Scripts are easy	→	The LCBS framework is efficient
Call high	→	Call appropriately

Prospecting is a process. Your goal is to be positively positioned on your VIPs' radar at the right time. This requires you to be willing to persist. And more importantly, to rethink *how* you persist.

3

ENGAGE

Take the Pest

Out of

Persistence

IF THE GOAL of prospecting is to be favorably positioned on my radar, then you need to actually *be* on my radar. Common sense.

So let's say you nail the first message by leveraging the LCBS framework, but the result is dead air. Nada. Eerie silence. What's startling in today's sales environment is how many sales pros believe that creating the right message will *guarantee* immediate access. And then they are bitterly disappointed when it doesn't happen, with most giving up after a second or third attempt.

Or maybe you do get a response. Yes!

But the client doesn't need you right now. Bummer!

We've all heard one or more of the following: "Check back with me in May." "We'll be issuing an RFP next year. Call me then." "Fire me a follow-up in six months."

Do *not* do as they ask.

Before you schedule a follow-up call four or five months into the future, consider this: The majority of buyers already have a preferred vendor in mind when they are ready to buy. Which suggests that you showing up months later is as naïve as hoping for a positive response to your wedding proposal on a first date.

This *inactive* time is your time to be *active*. You can turn dead air into an opportune selling time by using it to position yourself as #1 in the buyer's mind by the time she is ready to make a move. It's your time to drip gently on her consciousness. And when I say "drip" I am not referring to an annoying leaky-faucet drip. I mean drip relevance in a positive way that advances the sales process. Every interaction with your prospect during this time must contribute relevant value. If you prefer to take the easy route of simply "keeping in touch," then be prepared to join the large number of sellers who cross the line from persistence to irritation.

Remember, prospecting is not a one-time event. It's a process. And the process requires you to persist to get the results you are looking for. But there's a fine line between being persistent and being a pest. If your intent is to accelerate access (which I hope to heck it is), you don't want to cross that line.

Drip!

ONE OF MY BEST CLIENTS' first words to me were, "Jill, we're not looking for help with sales training." We had a brief conversation that provided me some background on the client and his team. Everything I heard screamed "VIP!" I was determined that when he was ready to buy, the two words in the bull's-eye of his radar screen would be sales and SHIFT.

And so I embarked on a personalized "drip" campaign. Think of this dripping as the sound of my relevance drowning out my competitors. Over the following months I used every sales channel available to me to follow up with this potential customer in appropriate ways relevant to him (I call this circling the wheel of prospecting, and we'll look at that in more detail in the "Circle the wheel of prospecting" section). Based on what I learned from our first conversation and subsequent industry research, I crafted messages that followed the LCBS framework. Always leading with the customer.

"I remember you saying you were looking for data on...," "You mentioned your team struggles with...," or "I read that your company is looking to..." I would lead with the customer's interests and then connect something of value—an article, a book, a useful statistic, a relevant success story from my own client base, and maybe even a little shameless promotion in the form of a testimonial from a client with a similar goal.

Drip. Drip. Drip.

Months into my campaign the call came in. My prospect was ready to engage. And the business was mine.

There's a fine line between persistence and stalking. The traditional campaign of e-mails that reiterate all of your fabulous features and benefits wears thin very quickly. Marketing guru David Newman sums this up with these words: "I don't get sick of hearing from you. I get sick of hearing from you about you."[1]

Equally annoying are: "I'm following up on my earlier e-mail," or "It's been a while and I just want to touch base," or "I'm just checking in." This is the common nonsense that defines insanity. Repeating self-serving prospecting messages multiple times and expecting a positive response is more likely to encourage the filing of a restraining order than the hitting of the reply button. You can get away with this generic approach once, but any more than that is lazy thinking and tells the buyer that you have nothing more to say than, "I want to sell you something that you probably don't need."

Here is one seller's fourth attempt in a string of identical "follow-up" e-mails. Although extremely polite, his message offers no trace of relevance to Douglas or his company.

> Good day, Douglas. Apologies if I am bothering you. I was wondering if my e-mails are reaching you. It would be really great if you can kindly acknowledge the receipt and let us know your thoughts. And also a good date and time that work well with your calendar for a brief discussion. Looking forward to your kind reply.

Douglas was kind enough to respond, but I'm guessing this wasn't the reaction this seller was aiming for:

> My thoughts are that it is more than a little presumptuous for a cold-calling e-mail string to escalate to a point where you imply I am rude for not acknowledging unsolicited sales calls. I do not need your services, and I "kindly" suggest you rethink your tactics.

The one-and-done approach to prospecting will leave you adrift in a sea of silence, waiting endlessly for a response that never comes. Conversely, inundating your prospects with irrelevant follow-up will do nothing but drown out the message you want to convey and dilute any chance of getting the business. Don't be a pest. Use the LCBS framework to drip relevant value over time to keep on your prospect's radar screen so that he turns to you first when he's ready to talk.

Fill your arsenal

THERE ARE MULTIPLE SITUATIONS where a drip campaign is called for:

- A prospect is not returning your e-mail or call.
- You've submitted a proposal, but your contact seems to have dropped into the abyss.
- You missed the mark in this year's bid process, and you want to be favorably positioned for next year.
- The client is happy with her current provider and, should circumstances change, you want her to think of you first.

Jennifer understood the value of the drip campaign as a differentiator. Her challenge: "Jill, I know I need to be in touch, and I know I need to contribute relevant value. But I get busy and run out of steam. Or more often I simply have nothing new to share."

My response to this dilemma: "Always know your *next action*. What you want to say, what you plan to send, and when you intend to act." To help me maintain the flow of relevant messaging to my VIPs, I turn to my access arsenal. This is a file (electronic and paper based) to which I regularly add items of high interest or value to my market. I'm always on the search for cool stuff to add, and I try to add new elements weekly. Building and maintaining your arsenal means you will never be paralyzed by "nothing new to share." It provides a constant source of ideas from which to create impactful sales messages. Here are some examples of what's housed in my arsenal:

- News about my VIPs' industries.
- Articles of specific interest to my markets.
- Statistics on sales performance and market trends. (Decision-makers value market data.)
- Links to non-competing expert videos.
- Thought-provoking questions and quotes.
- Past prospecting messages that have generated enthusiastic responses.
- Client testimonials. (My customers' words have more clout than mine.)
- Client success stories. (The proof to all of my promises.)
- Blog posts, tweets, and other social content—mine and that of other business experts.

I'll thoughtfully select what I plan to use with any given VIP and integrate it into the LCBS framework. I lead with their interests and connect specific content to these interests.

And I work smart. When selecting a specific item from my arsenal for one prospect, I consider who else on my list would benefit.

Filling your own sales arsenal with information relevant to your customers is an excellent way to build the evidence you need to access and engage with them. Update and purge the content of your arsenal often to keep it fresh, and you'll never be lost for words again. And the smartest thing you can do: Commit as a sales team to seeking and sharing content for a collective arsenal that helps everyone open doors.

Part two of Jennifer's struggle was: "How frequently should I drip?" and "When is enough enough?"

That depends. On the urgency from the prospect's point of view, the length of the sales cycle, the competitive situation. I don't want to hear from you every week if I am not planning to do anything for another year.

Your decision to throw in the towel or stay in the fray depends on many factors. The most important being: "Is this a VIP?" Some of my best clients have come through just when I am ready to let them go. In fact, many have thanked me for my tenacity. The information I've fed through on a regular basis has been the trigger that helped them to move sales training onto their front burner.

You don't want to follow the footsteps of the seller who had Douglas seeing red in the previous section. You want to be visible but not seen as a source of irritation. *How* you persist will dictate your client's perception. Remember LCBS relates to every interaction, and it will help you register on your VIP's radar more brightly than the pests.

Circle the wheel
of prospecting

HOW YOU PERSIST doesn't only relate to the content of your messages. How you *deliver* your painstakingly crafted messages, using multiple methods, will ensure your persistence hits pay dirt.

I was asked to present with sixteen other business experts in a summer-long webinar series covering a wide range of sales topics. Each expert was required to develop, present, and market their own forty-five-minute webinar, and to promote the entire series through their database. Registrants could pay for individual presentations or purchase the full series.

At the end of the summer, all of the presenters were asked to attend a virtual meeting to review the success of the program. I was surprised (and admittedly a little chuffed) to learn that my session drew six times more registrants than any other presenter's. It wasn't because my topic was stronger. Or that my name was a bigger draw. And we all had the exact same amount of time to market the program. So when the host asked me to share the specifics of my marketing campaign, my response was, "I didn't simply market the program. I sold it." And I sold it by circling the wheel of prospecting.

Many of my colleagues had relied on social channels to promote the series. They tweeted, blogged, and posted updates on LinkedIn. So did I. They used their chosen e-mail marketing platform to blast multiple messages to their entire database. So did I. They undoubtedly built awareness. But awareness does not deposit paid bodies in front of webinar screens. Selling does. Marketing talks to the masses. Selling is one to one.

In addition to my marketing activity, I also applied the uncommon sense of selling.

I defined my VIP in the context of this webinar series. Who would benefit most, specifically from a session on prospecting? Smaller companies who can't afford the high cost of on-site training. Larger companies with many "hunters" who prospect for their livelihood. Existing salesSHIFT clients who were due for a refresher on earlier training.

I combed my client list, my prospect database, and online networks looking for VIP sales leaders with the capacity to send me multiple candidates. I contacted VIPs who had expressed interest in hiring my company but had not yet done so. I offered this webinar as a cost-effective way to "take salesSHIFT for a test drive."

And then I dripped. I dripped using every element of the "wheel of prospecting."

I wrote personalized e-mails that followed the LCBS framework. I picked up the phone. And no, I didn't get a warm breathing body at the other end. I hit the inevitable voice mail every time. So I deposited evidence by applying... yes, you know it... the LCBS framework.

Every message, regardless of how it was delivered, clearly conveyed, "I am contacting you specifically because everything I know about you suggests this webinar will get you closer to your goals."

I put power in my messages by integrating objective educational statistics on the challenges of prospecting. I leveraged the horsepower of testimonials and referrals from raving fans who have heard me speak on the topic.

I contacted my network of suppliers, friends, and colleagues for their support in forwarding information to colleagues they knew would benefit from hearing about a webinar on this topic.

My goal was simple: a full house for my webinar on prospecting.

Persisting with relevant messages is one step to getting on your prospects' radar. Step two is being smart about how you deliver them. Circle the wheel of prospecting.

Many sellers favor one or two methods for delivering their prospecting messages. For many of my colleagues these are social media and e-mail. Both are vital elements of your prospecting strategy. But they are not the only ones available to you, and both deliver stronger results when used in conjunction with the other four approaches.

Using multiple methods in your prospecting activity is more effective than sticking to just one or two because different people respond to different approaches. It's also more interesting for the buyer, and for you, which will encourage you to persist. Regardless of the methods you use, the commandment that should guide your content remains consistent: LCBS. Lead, Connect, Be specific, and Say less.

And a word of caution: Adhering to this framework doesn't require you to lose your personality. Buyers are human beings. They want to hear from, buy from, and work with other human beings. People don't respond well to robotic scripts and perfectly crafted marketing pitches. Don't lose your humanity by over-formalizing or complicating your prospecting messages. The LCBS framework is the science of a good prospecting message, but the science without the art is like an Oreo cookie without the filling. It lacks the critical ingredient that makes it work: your individual personality and style. Humanizing prospecting is about being transparent, genuine, empathetic, and yes, even fun.

The next three sections introduce the uncommon sense of leveraging the six elements of the wheel to accelerate engagement of the right prospects.

E-mail and warm call, partners in prospecting

I'VE NOTICED THAT many sellers favor one or the other of the two longstanding prospecting methods: e-mail or the phone. Both continue to be relevant, provided you avoid the common nonsense that derails so many capable sellers and that you use them in partnership.

E-MAIL

Salespeople are addicted to e-mail. We are able to send one message to the masses with the click of a button. We don't feel pushy because we don't actually have to talk to anyone. And once we hit send, the ball is lobbed into the customer's court. The result: We just fooled ourselves into believing we are engaging a prospect and moving the sales process forward. If your sales cycle is limping along, it may be due to using e-mail as your prospecting crutch.

According to the Radicati Group, "Business e-mail will account for over 132 billion e-mail messages sent and received daily by the end of 2017."[2] Your important e-mail is now one of 132 billion. Poor odds for hitting my radar if this is your only method of delivery or if your message isn't carefully written to stand out.

In the sample e-mail that follows, Nick did a phenomenal job of following the LCBS framework while bringing his distinct personality to a creative and effective e-mail targeted at a specific audience: corporate meeting planners.

SUBJECT: Juggler wanted. Experience required.

Jill,

You'd be a perfect fit! It's a well-known fact that corporate planners are known for their ability to plan and execute multiple events over the course of a year. It's a tough job, and you're pulling it off, over and over again. Event planning is tough, period. But with those big revenue goals and tight budgets to deal with, many would argue that corporate meetings management is the most demanding of all.

So unless you'd like to take up juggling full-time, I'd love to show you how Cvent's Event Management platform can help you lose some stress, cut down on the mess in your office, and help you create more engaging, profitable events. How about lunch? I'll be in Toronto for a complimentary luncheon seminar and would love to have you join us. Below are the details.

...

Click here now to grab a seat. (Feel free to forward this invitation to your colleagues.)

In case you haven't heard about us, Cvent's event management platform is a one-stop solution for:

· venue selection and budget management
· online registration and payment processing
· e-mail marketing and social media engagement
· mobile apps for on-site check-in and attendee event guides
· event surveying and much more!

Like Nick, you can increase your odds of getting the right people's attention by crafting your e-mail to ensure the buyer is motivated to take three important steps:

Step 1. Open it.
Most sales e-mails are deleted without being opened. Your subject line matters. Personalize it, show relevant value, and pique my curiosity. Ideally all three, but at least one of the three. Oh, and keep it concise. Nick's e-mail sent to the corporate meeting planning community piqued my curiosity, and when I tested it on select members of his target audience, it had the same effect.

Step 2. Read it.
Too many sellers assume that a "catchy" subject line is enough. It's not. Think of the number of e-mails you open because of a clever subject line only to delete them as soon as you read the first narcissistic line. You want your e-mail read. Nick nailed it by *leading* with what is top of mind to the insanely busy meeting planner. He uses simple language to *connect* his benefits to seal the planner's interest. And the closing summary of his company's offering comes at a point where the reader is willing to digest it.

Step 3. Act on it.
Nick had a very specific request for action. An invitation to lunch with a direct link to RSVP. You want the reader to act on your e-mail.

Ultimately there are three possible actions:

- Respond.
- File for later.
- Delete.

While the first is your preferred reaction, there is also value in the second, provided you continue to execute your drip campaign to ensure that "filed" doesn't morph into forgotten. If you send an e-mail to a specific VIP, let them know that you also plan to take action. "Karen, I'll follow up with a call on Thursday. If you wish to connect before then, I may be reached at..." The knowledge that you don't plan to go away any time soon frequently triggers a response. Sure, it may be "Please don't bother to call me." But often I'll get, "Not a great time now, Jill. Give me a call in a couple of months." And yes, on occasion, they are at their desk prepared to talk when I call back.

And if you want your communications to prospects to stand out, don't forget that e-mail is not the only form of mail available to prospectors. While I receive over three hundred e-mails in any given day, I receive relatively few pieces of postal mail. And virtually no courier packages. Traditional mail still works, provided you use it in conjunction with other elements of the wheel and apply the LCBS framework to your messages.

WARM CALL

"No one picks up the phone these days!" You're right. The last statistic I read suggests that 80 percent of calls go straight to voice mail. So why bother? Here's why:

- Most prospects receive very few voice mails relative to the volume of e-mails.
- Most sellers choose not to leave a voice mail.

Therefore, a well-executed voice mail has a much greater chance of getting the receiver's attention, particularly if used in conjunction with other elements of the wheel. If you are one of the many who have discarded the phone as "dinosaur technology" and think that voice mail is for the birds, shift that thinking.

Consider the three choices you have when faced with voice mail.

1. **Do not leave a message.** Result: You don't exist.

2. **Leave an ill-prepared generic cold message.** Result: Delete.

3. **Leave a concise, conversational, personalized voice mail that follows the LCBS framework.** Result: You are on my radar.

Still wondering whether or not to leave a voice mail? Consider this: While you're hoping for that pipe dream possibility that your prospect is sitting by the phone ready to answer your call, a savvy competitor is leaving a smart message that puts them in the bull's-eye of your target VIP.

So get comfortable with the phone. Warm up your call with evidence that you've chosen to call me because you have something of relevant value. Know that I'll decide whether or not to listen to your message within the first five seconds. So lead with me and connect your value to my needs and interests. Cold calling, leaving a traditional benefit-choked message all about you, will prompt the wrong action—the pressing of the delete key. So remove "cold calling" from your prospecting vocabulary. Trish Bertuzzi sums up the reality of using the phone in today's world: "It is the cold that is dead. Not the calling."[3] Unless you are a telemarketer, there is zero excuse to cold call. Use all of the tips provided in this book to heat up your calls.

Don't fly solo

IT CAN BE EXHAUSTING having to continuously create compelling content for your sales messages. Smart sellers don't fly solo. They engage the support of others. The next three elements of the wheel of prospecting pump up the power of your messages by leveraging other resources.

EDU-SELL

Nobody wants to be sold. Buyers only want to hear from salespeople who contribute valuable insights pertaining specifically to their situation. So start "edu-selling." The internet provides a smorgasbord of educational content published by credible sources. Look to non-competing experts for rich content to add value to your messages. Seek out and share *prospect-relevant* articles, white papers, studies, video clips, and statistics—valuable market information that may not be readily available to your VIPs.

And don't discount your company's own intellectual property. When working with one client, I was dismayed to find that no one on his entire team of sales professionals had thought to read their own president's "state of the market" message in the company's annual report. A message that was chock full of educational data that could be masterfully integrated into the sales reps' prospecting messages. Apparently this is not uncommon. I have heard that almost a quarter of sales reps admit they don't read what their own company publishes.

When including these educational sound bites, don't

simply include an attachment or link. That reeks of laziness. Take it up a notch so that your message stands out from others. Demonstrate that you have thought about me and put thought into your message by using LCBS:

> Shauna, you immediately came to mind when my company published this post earlier this month. It touches on a subject important to the development of moldable, smart young sellers like your own, and it addresses your specific concern regarding the development of business acumen. Paragraph four points to an important role for your sales managers. I'll give you a call next week to see if we can provide any further guidance. If you wish to connect in the interim, I can be reached at...

REFERRAL

With distrust in the sales profession on the rise, buyers increasingly choose to listen to the words of other like-minded buyers over salespeople.

Referrals and testimonials are pure gold, so use them to help you shine. For example, Ellen referred me to the training director of a company that was looking to re-energize a very seasoned sales team, most of whom had been through an assortment of training programs over the years. Market conditions were rapidly changing. The team was not adapting. The current sales process was stale. I could have simply mentioned Ellen's name and hoped that its clout would trigger a positive response. But everyone does that, and it's not enough.

Before sending out an introductory e-mail, I quizzed Ellen on this company's situation and why she was suggesting I reach out to this contact. (I'll share more on how to do this in chapter 7.) Then I scoured my testimonial database. Rather than using my words to convince the client of salesSHIFT's fresh approach, I embedded the relevant and credible words of one of my earlier training participants in my e-mail. His words:

> I was less than enthusiastic to attend yet another sales training as this was probably the fifteenth throughout my career. Jill Harrington's qualities as a business person, a communicator, and seasoned sales leader quickly turned things around for me. Without question, one of the best trainers I've ever met.

And the door swung open. Never underestimate the power of your customer's words to move a prospect to act.

NETWORK

Every one of us has multiple networks. Online and offline: social networks, customers, suppliers, colleagues, friends, family, associations, and more. The question is, how proactively do you leverage each of these? I admit to needing to do a better job of this. Having a growing list of connections on LinkedIn is of zero value if you fail to tap into the networks of these warm contacts. And it doesn't stop there. At a Christmas party I tripped over the fact that one of my neighbors is a close friend of a prospect I had been trying to engage for years. You already know people with the connections to accelerate and simplify your prospecting efforts. You just need to engage their help. Share the key characteristics of your VIP profile with the people who want to see you succeed, and get others working with you to speed up the process of engaging the right prospects. Then return the favor. Offer your help to the people you admire and respect. That kind of good karma can pay big dividends to you down the line.

The final element of the wheel, social selling, is so important today it deserves its own private home in the book. It's also the source of the mistaken belief that selling today requires less effort and that fundamental sales skills are now superfluous. So this is where we're heading next.

Social sense

EVERY DAY I RECEIVE LinkedIn invitations from complete strangers from around the world. Why are they reaching out? It's not clear to me. And I'm pretty sure it's not clear to them.

No question, social media has revolutionized the sales process and transformed the way we communicate, learn, connect, and extend our reach. It's an incredible channel to help build awareness, earn trust, and engage new buyers in a sales conversation. Social selling is one spoke in the wheel of prospecting that accelerates your ability to build and strengthen credible relationships with the *right* prospects (your VIPs) and clients. It can position you to receive a warm welcome, rather than the cold shoulder, through the other prospecting channels.

Or not.

Because while social selling is the new darling of many salespeople, it's also a breeding ground for common nonsense.

I'm not going to provide a comprehensive list of the latest online tools and platforms. Nor am I going to write a lengthy chapter on how to use the most popular platforms. There's a long list of experts on the topic who are much better equipped to educate you. Instead, I've sought the advice and services of some of these specialists and, coupled with my own hits and misses, want to bring to you an important message along with three shifts that separate the social nonsense from the uncommon sense.

The important message comes from social evangelist Jill Rowley:

> "If you suck offline, you'll suck more online.
> Don't suck!"

Meaning: If it's not good practice in traditional ways of communicating, it sure as heck isn't good practice online. In fact, if you don't master the fundamentals of selling before unleashing yourself on the online universe, the results can be downright disastrous to your credibility. And ultimately to your sales career.

So here are my top three pearls of uncommon social sense.

THINK BEFORE YOU ACT

Social selling expert Jamie Shanks[4] refers to "activity for activity's sake" as the #1 example of common nonsense online. The first shift you need to make is moving away from random activity and toward a strategy that gets you active in the right places: where your buyers are. I've experimented with a number of social platforms, and I've narrowed my presence to three: LinkedIn, Twitter, and YouTube. This is my market's digital playground. So that's where I want to be. Get clear on yours, and then commit to continuous learning. There is no shortage of available expertise to help you create a strong social media presence in front of the people who matter most.

PUT THE ABCS ON STEROIDS

Social selling provides numerous avenues and opportunities to position yourself as a high-value resource to the right people. But remember, a self-serving pitch is just a pitch no matter how you deliver it. The foundational ABC, Always Be Contributing, is even more important online. Use multiple digital avenues to *contribute*. Post insights from within your organization and other expert resources. Craft thoughtful comments and responses to group discussions. Contribute only if you have something to add that enriches the discussion or provokes thought. Contribute to your customers' social success through likes, comments, and retweets of their important updates.

Social listening plants you firmly in your customers' shoes and provides an opportunity to take Always Be Curious to a whole new depth. The digital world presents a heaving buffet table to the curious seller. I like to stand on the sidelines watching and listening. I pick up on the persistent challenges and trends discussed daily within sales chat groups. I've learned more about client industry trends watching executive and expert videos online than from any other source. I get a sense of the interests of the companies and people with whom I want to engage by noticing what they choose to tweet and feature on their own profiles. All of this stokes the creative furnace to generate relevant evidence for future messages, posts, and introductory calls.

The final ABC, Always Be Connecting, is where many salespeople are most active online. If your purpose for connecting on LinkedIn is solely to build a mammoth list by firing out a barrage of generic invitations, then knock yourself out. But if your goal is to make a meaningful connection with a VIP or a person of influence within your VIP circles, you'd better put some thought into your request to join their professional network. When I receive the bland request to connect from a stranger, "Hi, Jill, I'd like to join your LinkedIn network," it triggers one word. "Why?"

Provide *evidence* up front that there is mutual value. It may be as simple as ego stroking: "Jill, I've been enjoying your articles and weekly Monday Motivations. I know others in my network will benefit from knowing you. I'd like to connect." You just got noticed because you led with information about me and connected something relevant to your request. You've done your homework and, hey, there's real value to having my writing exposed to a broader network. You've just made a connection in the true sense of the word. Now you can feel more comfortable firing out an InMail or even picking up the phone to ask for an introduction to others.

MANAGE YOUR PRESENCE

Given that most buyers conduct more than half of their research online *before* making an offline purchase, you want to be in their line of sight in the social media universe. If you've reached out to me, a buyer, via e-mail, phone, or another channel, and your message piques my interest, what do I do before I decide to respond? I visit your website, click onto your LinkedIn profile, and check out your social presence. And what will I find? Does your LinkedIn profile clearly articulate the value you bring to your clients or is it nothing more than a poorly crafted resume? Will I be pulled in? Or turned off? Does your social presence kill any chance of a conversation without you ever knowing?

While social selling doesn't *make* the sale—that rests firmly on your broad shoulders—it does advance the process of finding, understanding, and connecting with your VIPs. It helps you create personalized messages that cut through the clutter of today's sales environment. It enables you to convert a banal Unique Value Proposition into Value Propositions Unique to each VIP. It delivers an additional network of potential referrers to your doorstep. And it generates what every seller seeks: inbound leads. Used wisely, it can be one incredibly efficient sales channel to engage new buyers. Otherwise you're just another pest in cyberspace.

Eureka! A live one

GIVEN THAT SEEING BIGFOOT in Times Square seems more likely than a prospect actually answering their phone, many sellers neglect to prepare for the possibility that the prospect might just pick up. On the rare occasion that you get that unexpected "hello," it's as if Bigfoot himself has spoken. Rendering you speechless or, equally destructive, provoking a fast-flowing stream of "benefit babble."

Your ability to steady your emotions comes from how you've prepared before hitting the dial pad. Have you prepared the following?

- A concise conversational opening message that follows the LCBS framework.
- A handful of open-ended questions to engage the client, provoke thought, and pique interest.
- A handful of relevant and compelling insights you'll want to share in response to questions you anticipate the prospect will ask.
- Responses to difficult feedback, like "Who the heck are you?" "I don't have time right now." "We're not interested." "This isn't a priority for me." (You'll get help creating these in chapter 6.)

And when you get the coveted "Yes, let's meet," there's one remaining, often forgotten, step before you put it in your schedule. Learn from Dan:

Dan was thrilled when his prospecting efforts paid off and he managed to secure a meeting with a high-potential

VIP. I was excited for him. "Congratulations, Dan. So why did the customer take the meeting? What's he looking to get out of your time together?" Silence.

Like many, Dan had been so pumped to get a "yes" that his knee-jerk reaction was to schedule the meeting and get off the phone before the prospect changed his mind.

If I'm your prospect and I say, "Sure let's set up a time to talk," it means that something you said, or asked, caught my attention. You need to know what that is and why, so that you come to that hard-to-get meeting fully prepared to deliver on *my* expectations, not just yours. It's as simple as closing the conversation with "That's great, Jill. So that I make the best use of your time, is there anything specific on this issue you want me to be prepared to address? And what do you want to walk away with at the end of our meeting?" Asking for the client's expectation and desired outcome for a next meeting provides the following: information that allows you to prepare for a high-value and engaging first meeting from the customer's perspective, and a meeting that will move the sale forward.

Here's the other benefit of asking these questions before you hang up: You'll get a sense of whether there is legitimate interest, which increases the likelihood that the meeting will happen. You know that many first meetings end up being postponed. Indefinitely. Sometimes agreeing to a future meeting is a prospect's tactic to get a persistent seller off the line. It's easy to cancel at a later date. Frankly, it's a comfortable way for the buyer to say no. Remember, you may never get this person on the phone under this circumstance ever again. Always find out why the customer agrees to meet so that you can prepare to make this next interaction matter.

Make the shift

PERSISTENCE IS INTEGRAL to sales success. *How* you persist is what ensures a warm welcome and leads to faster results.

Mix it up! Use all spokes of the wheel to engage hard-to-reach prospects. Bring your own personal brand to each interaction. The one thing that doesn't change is LCBS: Lead with me to get my attention. Connect your value to seal my interest. Be specific because specifics sell. And Say less with more impact.

Be willing to execute your drip campaign. Build your drip campaign on the basis of Always Be Contributing relevant value so that you stand out as a trusted resource and are #1 when the time is right. Engage the support of your vast network of supporters and leverage the volume of customer data available on and offline.

Prospecting is a process. Avoid the common nonsense of giving up after two or three attempts. Engage the right prospects earlier so that you get into the game ahead of your competitors.

Common Nonsense → Uncommon Sense

Common Nonsense	Uncommon Sense
Follow up	Drip LCBS
Fire out repetitive messages	Leverage the content of your access arsenal
E-mail is king	Circle the wheel: use multiple methods
Social media requires less "selling"	The ABCs apply online
Fly solo	Engage the support of your networks
Hope for a live one	*Prepare* to maximize every live response

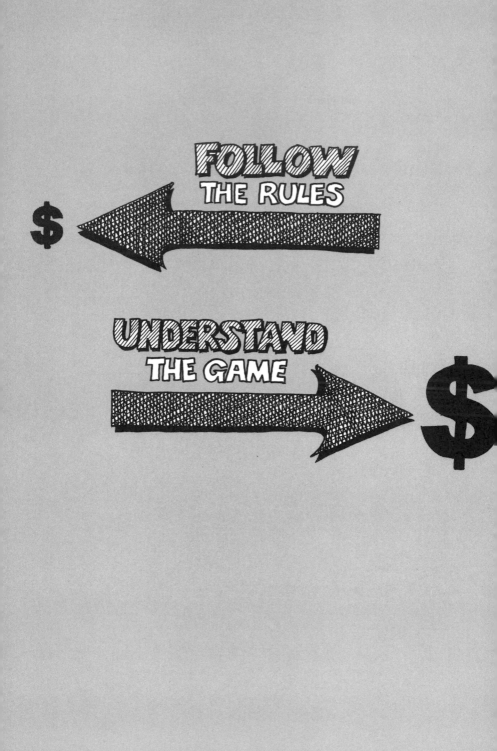

UNDERSTAND

Change the Rules

of the Game

for Bigger Wins

ONE OF THE MOST important wins of my entire career should never have happened. When I connected with Peter, the marketing director of an insurance company, he greeted me with disappointing news. "Jill, your timing stinks. We've just been through an extensive bid process with four of your competitors to decide who will manage our first annual broker incentive program. I just awarded the business to the winning company today. I'm sorry. Give me a call next year."

With no immediate opportunity on the table, I suggested an introductory meeting. "This is to be an annual event, and my company's expertise may be of value to you in future years. It's worth getting to know each other." He agreed. During our meeting we chatted briefly about the program he had selected for the coming year. Then we shifted the conversation to the business. We dug into one of the company's top priorities, a recent acquisition that was not delivering the planned results due to a disgruntled brokerage community. This critical sales channel was concerned about the fate of one of its local insurance suppliers, now absorbed into Peter's company, which was headquartered in a different province. The conversation suddenly had both of us questioning Peter's strategy for his first broker incentive program, although that had not been my intent.

During the bid process Peter had provided information to sellers from four different companies, and ultimately made his decision on the basis that this incentive program *needed* to compete with similar ones offered by other insurance providers in his market. His new realization: The program's #1 objective was to engage the support and loyalty of an important segment of the brokerage community and ensure the success of the acquisition investment. Peter now recognized that he had been about to apply a Band-Aid to a broken leg. And I had just changed the rules of the game.

Traditional needs-based selling (find a need, make a pitch) pulls sellers into the wrong game. Pursuing a need without the willingness to explore the bigger picture in collaboration with the customer is downright dangerous. In this case Peter had not yet signed the contract with my competitor. Our conversation led him to realize that he would benefit from seeing an alternate proposal. My company's recommendation was a full 180 degrees from Peter's original thinking. It hit the bull's-eye. So as my competitor was busy popping champagne over a verbal yes, I was signing the contract.

Be prepared to broaden the conversation. When making important decisions, buyers value a sales professional who has taken time to understand the *context* of their need—a seller who is willing to question, even challenge, their assumptions to get to the right solution. But remember, they are open to collaboratively changing the rules of the game if, and only if, it serves to benefit them.

The game-changing quadrants

FOR YEARS KEVIN'S company bid against the same four competitors on an annual multimillion-dollar contract. Every year his bid failed. He had assumed he and his competitors had an equal opportunity to win the business, but it turned out this client was using Kevin's lower pricing as a competitive benchmark. The client had no intention of awarding Kevin the business.

How do I know this? I was one of Kevin's competitors. I used the time between bids, when the client's purchasing executive was willing to spend a little time with me, to get a clear understanding of his buying process so that my company could better support it. I was able to uncover that two of the five bidders were not seen as viable contenders. Kevin's company was one of them. The client accepted the bid every year because Kevin requested the opportunity and his pricing was good. It helped them get a sense of market rates.

I knew Kevin's company. It was very capable. I thought about all the effort and expense that he and his sales team had put in over the years as they continued to march into the buyer's boardroom to present their recommendations, oblivious to the hopelessness of their bid.

How can you make sure you don't end up like Kevin, chasing business you have no chance of winning *and* being pulled away from other, better opportunities? Again, it's all about understanding the game you've entered and making sure you're able to compete on that playing field.

To define the game, you need to deepen your understanding of:

1. The client's business, and the market in which it operates.
2. The opportunity or need the client has communicated.
3. The buying situation. How this decision will be made.
4. The stakeholders. The people who influence, or are affected by, this decision.

I call these the four quadrants of discovery.

Use this tool to review what you know and what you need to know, and to formulate questions to fill in the gaps. The information you need and the questions you plan will depend on the situation and specific client opportunity. Some of this information you will uncover *before* you interact with the client, particularly in the business quadrant.

When a customer engages with a seller, he prepares to talk about what lies in quadrant #2, the opportunity. "I have a need. Looks like you might be able to help." Sellers arrive armed with a shopping list of questions to help them fully understand the stated need. That's important, but it's not enough. More business is won (or lost) as a result of information gained or missed in the other three quadrants: Q1 (the business), Q3 (the buying situation), and Q4 (the stakeholders).

Take my earlier example of the insurance company looking for a broker incentive supplier. My competitor had a surefire verbal agreement disappear before his eyes because his focus was 100 percent on the opportunity (Q2). It's only when I stepped back into Q1 (the business) that I found the real driver of Peter's company's decision to incent its sales channel. Only by having a broader conversation beyond the opportunity (need) itself did I find out that the recent acquisition was the top priority of the CEO, the most important stakeholder.

Similarly, Kevin's repeated inability to win in a competitive situation had nothing to do with the opportunity

THE FOUR QUADRANTS OF DISCOVERY

QUADRANT 1. THE BUSINESS	QUADRANT 2. THE OPPORTUNITY
Its market and key competitors. Its primary prospects and customers. Its point(s) of differentiation. Important products / services. Structure of the organization. Channels of distribution. Key executives / management. Organizational / departmental goals. a. How it plans to achieve these. b. Barriers and challenges to achievement. Trigger events.	Objectives of this initiative. Why and why now? Desired impact on the organization / division / people. Current state—history and levels of satisfaction. Key issues / challenges. Gaps. Desired state—what changes are needed and why. Definition / measures of success. Plans already in place. Current relationships. Specific logistical details.
QUADRANT 3. **THE BUYING SITUATION**	**QUADRANT 4.** **THE STAKEHOLDERS**
Drivers behind the need for change / this purchase. The decision-making process—step by step. Where the influence lies. Where the veto power lies. Who controls funding. Vendor selection criteria. Conditions under which they will: a. Select one vendor over another b. Keep the status quo c. Not proceed at all Our (the seller's) competition. And why. How the client plans to fund this initiative.	Information about the key decision influencers. Information about those impacted by the decision. In the context of this opportunity, what is most important to each stakeholder in terms of: a. Business outcomes b. Personal outcomes The vendor qualities that are most important to each stakeholder. Specific "management preferences." Stakeholder impressions of the various sellers, their company, and its services.

itself and everything to do with the perception of an influential stakeholder. If Kevin had been more curious about the buying process (Q3), had a tough conversation about why he continued to lose, and been open to hearing this primary influencer's perspective (Q4), he might have focused his attention on turning this misplaced opinion around— rather than investing time, money, and intellectual property on a bid that was doomed. Or he may have chosen to walk away from a resource-sucking process that was netting him nothing but grief.

A COLLEAGUE OF MINE was the underdog in a competitive bid against larger competitors. When he received the news that he was on the shortlist of two, he took a deeper dive into the buying situation and stakeholder quadrants. The clear message from his contact: "I have to take each vendor submission and net it down to present to my executive. At this stage all they want to know is this: What are we getting? And what are you charging? Terry, if you want to win this bid, make it easy for me to sell you to my boss."

Terry's competitor presented the traditional doorstop proposal filled with lengthy explanations, caveats, and disclaimers to their pricing. Terry went back to his team for input. They decided to play a different game. A more relevant game. Terry submitted two pages, a cover letter and a one-page business case for his team's recommendation. He spelled out exactly what his company would provide. At the bottom he submitted one fee. No hidden extras, no "subject to" clauses. Uncomplicated. Transparent. Relevant. He won. Was the format of his proposal the sole reason for the win? No. But Terry's exploration of the buying situation and his discovery of what was most important to these stakeholders enabled him to tailor his submission to their needs and, in his words, tipped the balance in his favor.

I have many stories of how sales professionals shift the rules of the game simply by uncovering important information. Information that others miss because they choose to focus their attention on the opportunity (Q2), only superficially skimming the other quadrants, if paying any attention to them at all. Go broad. Plan to explore all four quadrants. And, more importantly, *the relationship between the four.* This isn't about working harder than your competition to chase the opportunity; it's about working smarter to understand the full picture, get into the real game, and win bigger business.

The A in ABC

WE WERE ALL born curious. Then life happens. We gather experience. We become experts. We get busy with the urgent and lose sight of the important. And at times we become complacent.

I occasionally run workshops that require the sourcing of hotel meeting space. I'm fussy about the venue. Dark, musty meeting rooms suck the energy out of an audience. And me. A bright, tastefully appointed room energizes.

I had scheduled a site visit with a relatively new smaller hotel. A courteous hotel salesperson met me in the lobby, asked me about the specific logistical requirements for my group, and then walked me to the proposed meeting room.

Oh baby! Floor to ceiling windows spilling lots of natural light. Décor lifted right out of the pages of *House Beautiful* magazine. A perfect size. And because the property was new, a very fair rental rate. Sold!

My comment to the rep: "James, I had no idea this existed. You must be the best-kept secret in the city." His response? "Thank you, Jill." He then proceeded to show me the other facilities of the hotel. The gym. The pool. Because they were next on his site itinerary.

Now let's imagine the scenario if this hotelier had been curious beyond the immediate sale. If he had taken time to do a little homework on me before my arrival. If he had jumped on to the salesSHIFT website to understand who I am and what I do. If he had invited me to join his LinkedIn community and viewed some of my relevant connections.

And if he had used some of our walk-and-talk time to explore my professional background. If James had shown a greater interest in the human being viewing his property, he would have discovered the following:

1. **I have several clients in the local business community and am involved with a handful of associations that run regular meetings.** All potential clients for James.

2. **My network includes a vast number of local professionals who plan and execute corporate meetings.** Potential clients for James.

3. **I know scores of trainers and consultants who use hotel function space for client meetings and seminars.** Potential clients for James.

Imagine where the conversation might have traveled if James had been curious. Armed with these insights, his response to my comment, "You must be the best-kept secret," might have been smarter. "Thanks for the compliment, Jill. Frankly, we don't want to be a best-kept secret. Given what I've read about your involvement in the meetings industry and what you've shared with me this morning, perhaps you know of others who would benefit from hearing about us."

Had James shifted from his traditional site visit agenda to a place of genuine curiosity before, during, and even after this encounter with a new client, he might have walked away with more than this one small gig. This approach might have resulted in a valuable long-term relationship and multiple qualified business introductions.

Always Be Curious. This game-changing mind-set ensures that you'll have more productive customer interactions. And I mean more productive for both you and the buyer.

Curiosity starts long before a client interaction. It used to be that sales pros relied on a first meeting for an opening to get curious. Today sellers need to get curious in order to snag that first meeting. We live in an age where we can access market and client data by following people and companies on social platforms or have it delivered directly to our inboxes through Google Alerts and subscriptions to industry blogs and groups. There's no excuse, other than laziness or lack of interest, for neglecting this ABC early in the process. And consider this: 99 percent of customers want sellers to come to a first meeting well prepared and with knowledge of their business and industry. Yet only 11 percent of buyers are satisfied with their first meetings with vendors.[1] Translation: Doing your homework is a big fat opportunity for you to stand apart from your competitors. And to shift those rules.

This game-changing ABC needs to continue through every step in the sales process. I encourage sales pros to make a point of learning something new about their client in *every* single interaction, whether it's a presentation, a phone call, a lunch, even a golf game. It's shocking how many opportunities to deepen our understanding go missed.

Deidre and her team had a full hour to present to a room of potential buyers. Within twenty minutes, the presentation was finished. The team offered to take questions, but there were none. The clients returned to their desks, and Deidre's team was left alone with an empty box of donuts and forty minutes of dead air in which to ponder, "What just happened?"

Forty minutes of quality time with high-potential buyers gone. A once-in-a-lifetime opportunity missed. That's what happened.

There were a number of factors that led to this disappointing outcome, not the least of which was inadequate preparation for an hour-long meeting. But the opportunity may have been salvaged if the team had remembered the A in Always Be Curious.

In this case Deidre and her team came to present their capabilities. They simply didn't think to use this gift of time to turn the tables and learn about their audience: "We have some time left, so we'd like to take a few minutes to listen to you. We're extremely interested in getting your feedback. In particular we'd love to hear your perspective on what's trending in your market and how organizations like ours can better support your success."

This meeting could easily have run the full hour. It could have afforded the selling team an opportunity to deepen their relationship with eight high-influence buyers and provided game-changing information that would enable them to continue to contribute relevant value through a thoughtful drip campaign after the meeting. They might also have uncovered an opportunity that the client had not thought to share at first.

Curiosity isn't just for before and during meetings. It needs to continue after your client interactions.

I had met with a VP looking for an expert to keynote her national sales conference. The VP shared her deep concern about sales rep morale. The company was going through a major rebranding. This upgrade was about to drive up prices and push some of their hard-earned and loyal clients into the eager arms of cheaper competitors. The repositioning was also pushing the sales reps out of their comfort zone and requiring them to engage with a different breed of buyer.

After I left the meeting, I scheduled time with some of the reps. I was curious to get their first-hand perspectives. Nerves were frayed. Some feared for their jobs. Others questioned their personal ability to make the leap. This additional information and perspective enabled me to build a proposal that was very different from those submitted by my two competitors. One that got me the win at 160 percent of the original budget. My proposal didn't dwell on the specific content of my keynote presentation. Rather, I focused on the client's critical goals for this "once-in-a-lifetime conference," and on specifically how we would use the opening session as the catalyst for shifting the sales reps' fears into confidence.

Curiosity is not something to be switched on and off, but rather a constant state of mind. The A in Always Be Curious will help you develop a winning attitude that enables you to write efficient access messages, develop attention-grabbing drip campaigns, and enter your client meetings ahead of your competitors. Just one word of caution: Never confuse "Always Be Curious" with the common nonsense of "Ask more probing questions."

Stop probing!

EVERY TIME I HEAR the word "probe" I'm haunted by a visual of some distasteful medical procedure that most of us would choose to avoid. Seriously... who wants to be probed?

Yet "Ask more probing questions" is a directive barked by well-meaning managers and trainers to encourage the "how" of curiosity. And it needs to be permanently laid to rest right next to Always Be Closing because buyers are sick of answering an interminable list of fact-finding questions. Three sellers into the process, this approach has the buyer looking for the nearest sharp object to drive into her skull. It stalls rather than advances the sales process. No wonder so many buyers choose to protect their sanity by using e-mail and RFPs to hold this onslaught of seller-focused questions at arm's length.

So here's the uncommon sense. Stop probing!

Instead, ask *fewer, smarter* questions, *in context*. The *right* questions that serve both the client and the seller. Questions that provoke thought, pique interest, and encourage engagement in a business dialogue. Leverage the information you have gathered before your meeting to enter the conversation with a healthy EiQ.

Educated insight + Question = EiQ

We've never had such easy access to important insights about our clients, their business, and their markets. Social media profiles, posts and tweets, blogs and videos, websites, news releases, investor reports, association white papers, publications, people. The Ei of EiQ is at our fingertips. Many sellers I know are doing their homework, but they often fail to leverage these insights to ask better questions. Let me give you a couple of examples where the traditional question sounds seller-focused but embedding a little Ei in the Q serves the client *and* enhances the seller's credibility. You be the judge.

Traditional probing question: "What is your budget?"

EiQ: "In our experience, smaller associations are working with tight budgets, which often requires them to find creative sources of funding. How do you plan to fund this initiative?"

The second question clearly demonstrates your understanding of the client's industry. The reference to others sourcing creative funding triggers a different thought process. And a different conversation, one that can shift the client away from focusing on the restriction of a fixed budget. You can step into the conversation as an expert who can provide proven alternatives to traditional funding options.

Here's another example.

Traditional probing question: "Who is the decision-maker?" Some buyers avoid answering this. They hear, "I want to know so that I may stalk the boss." I've seen others take offence, interpreting this query as, "You are attempting to bypass me. Obviously I'm not important to you." Plus, this question doesn't unearth the information most valuable to you. Ideally you want to understand the full process for the decision and where the points of influence lie.

EiQ: "It sounds like this is one of your top two initiatives for this fiscal, and you need to get this right. What is your process for ensuring you get to the right decision?"

This approach demonstrates that you understand the importance of this person's mandate and that you appreciate the significance of this initiative. It's a gentle reminder to your contact that this should not be a quick decision. Focusing your question on the process, rather than on one person within it, will provide a more comprehensive picture of the decision-making process, including the various points of influence up to the decision-maker. You can then take a deeper dive to explore each of the important stakeholders' interests.

Use your EiQ within the conversation. Listen and leverage important client input to deepen your understanding and your engagement with the buyer. "Alma, you've mentioned your president a few times. It sounds like this initiative is high on his agenda. Can you share a little more about his specific interests and involvement?"

Leveraging your EiQ to position your questions in the context of the buyer's interests leads to a stronger conversation. Your questions land differently with the buyer because they make her think. That's what I want from a salesperson.

I want an expert to hold up a mirror to bring greater clarity to my situation. *Stretch my thinking.* I don't need to spend time with a warm body firing a list of probing questions that are intended to do nothing more than sell me something.

Every sales expert talks about the importance of asking questions. Taken at its most literal, that advice is driving nonsensical, even irritating, behavior. Customers don't want to be probed for what's important to *you*. Probing shuts down the possibility of any broader conversation and puts you on the road to commoditization because you sound like your competitors. Using your EiQ generates a warmer response, uncovers higher-quality information, and starts the differentiation journey.

Can you hear me?

I LOST MY VOICE in 2012. The combination of a viral infection and an overambitious speaking schedule resulted in swollen vocal cords and strict orders from the ear, nose, and throat specialist to rest my voice. Considering the only sound I was able to make was an incomprehensible rasp that made Marlon Brando's Godfather sound like the soprano in a children's choir... I really had no option.

For several weeks my only means of face-to-face communication was to hold up furiously scribbled notes. Usually by the time I had penned my witty response, the conversation had moved on and I was no longer a participant in the dialogue. I eventually resigned myself to my new—and challenging—role. That of mute observer and listener.

Here's what I noticed:

- People frequently interrupt each other or unconsciously finish each other's sentences and, as a result, never get to hear what the other person planned to say.
- Two people are very capable of carrying on a "conversation" without actually hearing what the other says.
- People love to talk about their own perspective and assume others love to hear it.
- Human beings quickly withdraw from a conversation when they don't feel heard.

Few human beings are excellent listeners. Salespeople, according to many customer surveys, stink at it. We try to be attentive, but we're at a disadvantage because our brains are governed by our perspectives (our service will make you money, so you'd be crazy not to talk to us), our beliefs (we really do have a better service than your current provider), or our agenda (I need to close one new account before month end). We become the proverbial solution looking for a problem.

IT IS LITTLE WONDER sellers fail to hone their listening skills, given how much time is focused on teaching sales professionals how to talk: to craft elaborate benefit statements, deliver persuasive presentations, and create show-stopping responses to client objections. We've got this all wrong; *hearing* our customers is a skill that is foundational to changing the rules of the game so you can win big.

David Schwartz says it best: "Listening means letting what's said penetrate your mind. So often people pretend to listen . . . they're just waiting for the other person to pause so they can take over the talking. Concentrate on what the other person says. Evaluate it."[2]

Effective listening is about how we hear or interpret the meaning behind others' words. Are we creating meaning from our seller's perspective? Or are we exploring the meaning by the customer's definition?

Here's a recent example:

Client: "We've been trying to push this initiative forward for a long time. I think we finally have the executive team on board, so we should be able to move forward."

Through the salesperson's filter it sounded like this, "We've got the green light. We're ready to buy."

But the customer's statement is loaded with implication. That necessitates the deep dive of curiosity.

"We've been *trying* to push this initiative forward for a *long time.*"

Why hasn't the executive team been behind this initiative in the past? What's been the holdup? The answers will provide clues to potential barriers, some of which may still be lurking.

And what has shifted the interest of the executive? If the contact fails to provide a convincing answer, I'd want to explore further.

"I *think* we finally have the executive team on board."

Either they think or they know. You want the latter. Get them to elaborate on their "thinking."

"We *should* be able to move forward."

Ask the important question: "What will it take to have your executive 100 percent behind this and championing the move forward?"

By listening for meaning and being curious about the implication, you are not only finding out if this is a genuine opportunity. You're also helping your contact understand the executive team's position more clearly, which might help them avoid a crushing disappointment.

Listening skills often go missing in action when you're faced with a client who disagrees with your expert input or offers an opinion that conflicts with your own. So here's the important question for you. Are you able to shift from a mind-set of judgment to curiosity? To willingly explore this opposite point of view? Or do you subconsciously filter their words to hear what you choose to hear? Worse still, do you immediately jump to defend your own position, causing the client to withdraw?

Most importantly, are you able to refrain from giving your point of view until others have shared theirs fully, so that when you speak you do so with more impact? I recall a senior strategy meeting that went around in circles, with each executive jumping on the words of their colleagues, determined to have their say. Except for one who remained silent. When the rest of us were done, he simply said, "After listening to everyone's opinion on the matter, I have just three things to say…" His three points, shared in under two minutes, were more insightful than the two previous hours of talking.

Listen as if the other person's perspective matters. Because it does. Not only does the act of hearing your customer help you take away accurate information to qualify an opportunity and serve as the bull's-eye for your proposal, but when people feel heard and deeply understood, they share more. And that's game changing.

Ask the
tough questions

AFTER MONTHS OF calling, I finally got the nod from Eric, the VP of a large manufacturing company, to be part of an upcoming bid process. Up until this point he had kept me at a distance, and for a valid reason: He was extremely happy with his current provider. Persistence had paid off in terms of gaining me access this year, but there was no guarantee of a sale. We had a good and thorough conversation. Eric was open. I liked him. I wanted to work with him. But something was niggling at me. I heard no compelling evidence to suggest that he was ready to switch to a new supplier.

"Eric, this has been fun. I have enjoyed getting to know you. I appreciate your time, and I'd love to work with you, but I have a question, and I'm going to be blunt. I'd appreciate the same candor back from you. You have a long-term incumbent with whom you're obviously very satisfied. Is there any reason why you'd switch next year?"

Silence. I could tell he was mulling his response. And then the honest answer I'd requested, straight back at me. "No."

Bottom line: This year Eric was required by his company to go to bid. His current provider would have to "really screw up" to lose this contract. Neither of us saw that happening. So there it was. The big fat gnarly elephant in the room, fully exposed. Not the answer I wanted to hear, but better that than some polite fib to spare my feelings.

When I share this story with others, many say they would not have asked the question for fear it would prompt the client to realize there is no reason to switch. Utter nonsense. If it was on my mind, Eric was already thinking it. Other sellers might choose to filter Eric's words and plow forward in the rose-colored haze of conviction that they are better than his current partner and can win the business. But that's just not smart.

Eric's answer enabled me to make an important decision with twenty-twenty vision: Continue with the bid or walk away. I chose to bid that year and I didn't win; he retained his incumbent. I went ahead with eyes wide open and decided to submit my proposal knowing it was a long shot. But it was one I was prepared to take on this occasion because of the opportunity to showcase our capabilities to a client who aligned with my VIP profile. In this case I was willing to be in the #2 position on Eric's radar in the event that something changes in the future. This decision was based on the facts and not colored by naïve optimism.

THERE ARE ALL KINDS of situations that require us to step up our game and ask the tough question.

Remember Kevin from earlier in this chapter, who was bidding for the same business every year and losing? He was long overdue for asking the tough question, "Can we talk candidly about why we are bidding every year and failing to provide what you need?" This direct line of inquiry would give the customer permission to skip the BS and give the straight goods. And it might free Kevin up to move on to other opportunities better suited to him and his company, rather than playing a game he can't win.

Have you ever lost to the status quo? "Almost one-quarter of forecasted sales deals result in no decision."[3] This suggests the status quo is one of your most formidable competitors. If you're having a discovery conversation and you're wondering why a customer with adequate resources doesn't manage this project in-house, guess what? So is someone inside the company. Use your EiQ to position the tough question so that it is easy to answer. For example, "Given the depth of expertise within your own marketing department, I'm curious to know if you considered handling this initiative in-house?" or "Can we talk a little more about your decision to outsource this year?" If their reasoning is weak, that's a big red flag.

Not every opportunity is the right fit for you. Don't be an ostrich; get your head out of the sand and ask the tough questions. Don't be so blinkered by the potential sale that you miss clues that this might be a dead end. Do not be so deafened by the trumpet of an impending win that you discount the perspective of a key stakeholder who might torpedo the whole deal. Set aside this common nonsense and be brave enough to ask the tough questions. As hard as the answers may be to hear, they can save you from running into a brick wall of frustration and help you shift your focus to better opportunities.

Make the shift

WE ALL KNOW the tragic fate of the *Titanic*. The revolutionary new passenger ship collided with an iceberg, and in less than three hours this "unsinkable" vessel was below water, leaving over 1,500 people dead.

It was not the 10 percent of the ice mass seen by the crew that precipitated the most deadly peacetime maritime disaster in history. It was the 90 percent that was out of sight, the breadth and depth below the waterline, that crushed the starboard side, caused it to fill with water, and sealed the fate of the *Titanic* over one hundred years ago.

Now think about this. When a customer provides you information, he is giving you what he believes you need to come back to him with a workable solution. He is giving you the view from "above the waterline." But if you are relying exclusively on the information provided by the customer, or using traditional questions to gather information, you are cruising on the water, able to see only 10 percent of the situation, and heading into dangerous waters.

Add to that the liability of expertise. Over one hundred years ago, expert shipbuilders made the assumption this remarkable ship was unsinkable. As a result they equipped it with lifeboats to hold just one-third of the full passenger capacity. Similarly, our expertise as salespeople can lead us to make assumptions that can take us down the wrong path, a path to a dead end rather than to the win.

Many people say that information is power. When it comes to selling, I disagree. What gives you power in selling, and ultimately enables you to change the rules of the game so that you are not competing head to head, is the *quality* of information you acquire, *when* you acquire it, and *how* you use it. In short, the game changer in selling is your willingness to Always Be Curious.

It's the 90 percent you don't know that will ultimately sink you. And it takes work to expose the 90 percent. Ninety percent of the information you need lies predominantly in the three game-changing quadrants (Q1, Q3, Q4). Within this vast hidden cache of information lies your opportunity to shift the rules of the game. And to differentiate yourself, your company, and your offering from the pack of sellers vying for this sale and for a bigger business relationship with the client. Understanding your customer and their whole situation fully will ultimately position you to win a bigger game.

Common Nonsense ➡ Uncommon Sense

Common Nonsense		Uncommon Sense
Information is power	→	The *right* information powers the winning game
Ask more probing questions	→	Ask fewer but smarter questions in context (EiQ)
Explore the opportunity	→	Explore all game-changing quadrants
Curiosity happens when you're with the customer	→	The A (Always) in Always Be Curious is the game changer
Listen to the customer's words	→	Hear the meaning and implication behind the words
Focus on the 10 percent	→	Seek out the 90 percent

POSITION

Make It

Easy to Choose

You

I WAS AT THE BACK of a corporate boardroom observing eight hotel sales managers, representing different cities around the world, present their individual properties to a room of ten strategic hotel-room buyers.

Following introductory comments from the regional director, each member of the team got seven minutes to present their hotel and explain why it met the interests of the very lucrative corporate group market.

Each of the eight presenters was professional, charismatic, and knowledgeable—but one magnetized the room. When I spoke privately with members of the audience, the response was consistent: "We like these guys. But this was the typical 'spray and pray' presentation. Spray us with information and pray we buy. With the exception of Lynne."

Seven of the eight hospitality sales managers presented what they believed to be important to their audience. Their hotel's central location, which was close to shopping, restaurants, and major points of interest. The quality of their restaurant. The unique group function space. All important attributes. However, by presenter number four, we were hard pressed to remember, or distinguish between, the presenters and their individual hotels.

Lynne positioned her hotel *in the context* of her audience. She led with her understanding of this market. Busy event planners. Creative minds. Canadians.

She had listened for meaning in the earlier introductions and referred to her clients' words. "You mentioned that Canadian groups are typically smaller than their US counterparts, but they don't want to feel less important." Lynne made the connection between the size of her boutique hotel in a city of mega-resorts and the customers' preferences, guaranteeing "your smaller group will be the big fish in our small pond." "The presence of a larger sister resort across the street," she added, "accommodates those who want the 'bells and whistles' facilities of a big resort."

She acknowledged her understanding that event planners work exceptionally long days on-site with their groups, constantly juggling unanticipated changes and last-minute requests on an hour-by-hour basis. She explained that her hotel's non-unionized status means, "Unlike other hotels that must wait for the appropriate unionized personnel, we have the ability to respond immediately to your needs, making your life easier, getting things done faster, and keeping your customers happier."

She did not talk about her "unique function space," she placed us in it. She painted a vivid picture of a recent group's evening welcome reception in the penthouse bar, where floor to ceiling windows had the group "floating" high above the lights of the downtown strip below. By telling a story, she engaged our emotions as well as our thinking.

Simon Sinek says it best: "There's barely a product or service on the market today that customers can't buy from someone else for about the same price, about the same quality, about the same level of service and about the same features."[1] Translation: Product, brand, and service features no longer sell. Presenting information on its own makes you indistinguishable. How you position the relevant attributes of your brand, product, or service; how you position your organization in the context of what your customer cares about most. That's what sells.

In chapter 2, I introduced you to the positioning framework LCBS, which is your prospecting gas pedal, accelerating your access to good prospects. As we progress though the sales cycle, this powerful formula turbocharges the impact of your client presentations and proposals.

Lynne stood out because she used the LCBS framework to position her hotel to win.

Turbocharge your presentations and proposals

YOU WORK HARD to gain access to, engage, and understand your potential new clients. Presentations, proposals, meetings, and demos are valuable sales tools that will lead you to the winner's circle—provided you don't default to the common nonsense of enthusiastically gushing everything about you that's not that important to me, which ultimately kills any hope of differentiating you.

I've beaten you over the head with the importance of making the connection between relevant attributes of your offering and the customer's priority interests. Why? Because most sellers believe they do a good job of this. Yet according to the buying community, we don't. While 71 percent of sellers believe they tailor their pitch to the customer's needs, a mere 37 percent of buyers agree.[2] Now if that's not evidence that a large chunk of the sales profession is sporting a heavy set of blinkers, I don't know what it is.

Hit the pause button and take a look at your own proposals and presentations. What's the content of the first page of your proposal or the opening statement of your presentation? Who are you leading with? You? Or your client? Now I'm not suggesting that this is an invitation to regurgitate everything the client already knows about herself, unless your goal is to put her to sleep. Rather, leading with the customer's interest is your opportunity to demonstrate your accurate understanding of who she is, her situation, the drivers behind her need for change, and the reasons she's agreed to invest time listening to you, reading your proposal, or responding to your e-mail. This is the bull's-eye for what will follow. It dictates what you will share in your meeting, presentation, or proposal.

Next question. Do you make clear "hit the client over the head" connections between the attributes of your offering and the customer's desired outcomes? Or have you assumed the buyer will make the connection? Most buyers don't. It's your job to connect the dots—with a neon yellow pen. When you articulate clear connections, the customer hears them differently than if they make them themselves. The result: You stand out.

Consider Lynne's example in the previous section. She didn't simply include her non-union status in a list of her property's attributes. She made important connections between that feature and its impact on the buyer. A feature that, as she pointed out, would help minimize the stress and craziness of their jobs. She answered two important questions.

1. How?

She clearly articulated "how" the non-union attribute of her hotel alleviates the planners' stress by enabling a faster response to the unexpected.

2. So what?

She connected this faster response back to the impact on the planners' clients. Faster responses lead to happier and more impressed clients. She could even have taken it one step further: "Impressed clients become repeat clients, and your potential referrers. All of which ultimately contributes to the growth of your business."

In contrast, Lynne's peers delivered a shopping list of generalizations and lost the audience's full attention. Lynne differentiated herself by selecting three relevant attributes of her hotel and speaking *specifically* about how each feature added value for this audience. As a result Lynne was able to *say less* with considerably more impact. Leaving her time to engage her audience in further dialogue. And making her short presentation memorable.

Be the obvious choice

AS SOMEONE WHO reviews sales proposals, sits at the back of presentations, and reads a ridiculous number of prospecting messages, I have a simple observation: Many of you are making your customers work way too hard to get what they need from you. In short, you are making it difficult for them to choose you.

It goes back to our discussion on game-changing data. Information is power only if you use it selectively to position yourself to be the most relevant seller to the customer—the obvious choice.

So when preparing for your proposal, presentation, or conversation, go back to the information you gleaned in each of the four quadrants of discovery. Then, ruthlessly and relentlessly plan to make connections between what you offer and the customer's priorities.

Here's a simple approach I call the "center-line test" that helps ensure you make these vital connections. Review your discovery notes. Create two columns by drawing a line down the center of the page or creating a two-column table on your screen. In the left-hand column, capture the critical interests of your customer from each of the four quadrants of discovery. Use their words wherever possible.

Q1: The business outcomes they seek.
Q2: The opportunity specifications.
Q3: The criteria and process for making the decision.
Q4: The interests and preferences of key stakeholders.

In the right-hand column, beside each client interest, answer this question: *How* are we addressing this? The "how" may be a specific attribute of your offering, or it may be a relevant attribute of your company. It may be an area of expertise you personally bring to this situation.

Here's what you're preparing to say throughout your proposal. "Mr. Customer, here's the issue, problem, or challenge you shared. And here's specifically *how* this component of our solution will address it." A customer priority in the left-hand column without value connected to it from the right equates to seller vulnerability.

Now step out of your own shoes and into those of the various stakeholders who will read your proposal or attend your presentation. Standing squarely in each influencer's shoes, ask yourself, "Have I made clear connections to what this person seeks? Have I articulated a sparklingly clear vision from the customer's perspective as to *how* we will resolve each of her priorities? And *how* it will get her to her ultimate business goals?"

Remember Terry from chapter 4? He's the sales pro who found game-changing information in Q3 (the buying situation) and Q4 (the stakeholders). He heard that the key stakeholders were not prepared to wade through pages of irrelevant data to cull what was needed to make a smart decision. Terry's one-page business case beat out the lengthier competitive proposal because Terry made it easy for this contact to sell Terry internally. Terry didn't hide his relevance in an encyclopedic listing of everything the executive didn't need to make a good decision.

While Terry's one-pager was a success in this instance, more often we need to provide a comprehensive proposal. Which is why the executive summary is an essential element of any submission. Given that this may be the only page read by high-level decision-makers, here is where you want to be ruthless in your application of the center-line test to make crystal-clear connections between your recommendations and the client's strategic priorities. And remember, the addendum is the place to put everything that's useful for stakeholders to know but not integral to the decision-makers' process.

Buying decisions have become increasingly complex, involving multiple people, most of whom are attempting to keep many balls in the air. Much of the selling occurs without you being present to guide behind-the-scenes stakeholders through the merits of your proposal. So any connections between the customer's interests and your offering are, therefore, at risk of getting lost. Unless you spell them out.

Proposals are not marketing vehicles. They are important sales tools intended to help buyers make good decisions. Content is important. But content doesn't guarantee the win. Put your content in the context of what's important to each specific buyer. In a world where information has become a commodity, relevance wins.

The tragedy today is that proposals with good content are losing because not enough thought is put into who is reading the document or how it will be read. Decisions are frequently made by teams. Will each member of the team read your entire proposal or will each be allocated one element to review? The latter requires you to think deeply about each section of your proposal and about the message and connections that must thread through each page.

Meticulously following the LCBS framework makes it easy for your potential client to do business with you—whether you're in the room to make the sale or not.

L: Lead with the customer's interests.

C: Connect your value.

B: Be specific.

S: Say less with more impact.

The discipline
of less

THIS TIME I AM observing a thirty-minute presentation that a seasoned technology sales rep is making to a group of fourteen resellers. These are the people who can provide him with immediate access to multiple clients across North America. He has thirty minutes, and he is about to blow an opportunity of a lifetime.

After a few minutes of pre-presentation chat, the presenter launches into an unstructured information stream accompanied by a series of busy slides. Twenty-five minutes in, he knows he is running out of time. Rather than cutting to the chase to make his overarching point, he moves to a strategy of "talk and click faster" to finish the full Power-Point deck supplied by his marketing department. At the thirty-minute mark, now officially out of time, he shifts to the infamous Energizer Bunny approach. He just keeps on going. Eventually the remarkably patient host stands, calls "time," and cuts off the flustered presenter mid-sentence, finally putting this important audience out of its misery.

What a tragic waste of time, money, and business opportunity for both the presenter and the audience.

Now, you may be thinking that this is an extreme example; professionals don't do this. Think again. Professional sellers don't intentionally do this. But sometimes the busyness of life, the complacency of experience, or our enthusiasm to share it all kicks common sense out of the door.

Consider this: In a four-year time period, customer dis-satisfaction with proposal presentations has increased by 13 percent. And 51 percent of buyers want presentations to be shorter and more comprehensible.[3] When it comes to sales, less really is more. Easy to say; hard to do.

To make an indelible impression with an important audi-ence within a short time frame, you have to think deeply about what you plan to say. *And what to leave out.* Choose fewer points. Focus on the specific aspects of your product, service, or solution that are relevant to this audience rather than trying to cover every feature, specification, and detail. The audience in this situation needed three important ques-tions answered:

1. **What issues does your technology address for the end customer we serve?**
2. **Why should our customers use your technology versus the alternatives?**
3. **What's in it for me to promote your product to my customer base?**

This vendor could have avoided suicide by PowerPoint by coming armed with a handful of simple visuals that directly addressed these three points instead of doing an informa-tion dump and using his visuals as a crutch for his words. He might have held his audience's attention if he had put a little thought into their interests, their desired output from this investment of precious time, and the fastest route to get there.

You may have heard this advice: "If you have sixty min-utes to make a point, take forty minutes to plan it and twenty minutes to say it." These words are more relevant than ever. We live in a world of the gnat-like attention span. Despite your enthusiasm, the kitchen sink does not belong in your sales messages, presentations, or proposals. Buyers don't hear what you tell them; they hear what they need to hear—the stuff that's relevant to their end goal and decision path. Sadly, the points of greatest value to them may get drowned out by the muddy waters of information overload. Discard unnecessary data. Eliminate fluff so that every word counts. And connect everything back to your specific audience's interests.

Use handouts, links, or whatever is appropriate to share the additional elements you *want* to share, but don't let what you want to share get in the way of what they *need* to know.

Give your words a little CPR

BY LEADING WITH the customer's words and connecting your value, the LCBS framework puts your customer at the heart of the conversation. The power of positioning, putting your content in the context of what the customer cares about most, goes beyond prospecting messages, presentations, and proposals.

A group of sales reps was discussing the struggle to articulate a concise response to the question, "What does your organization do?" Isaac kindly offered to share his company's elevator pitch. Ninety seconds in, I looked around the room. A sea of blank faces.

I detest the term "elevator pitch." Firstly, it makes me think of an elevator. How is that useful? And pitch? Every time I hear the p-word I think of snake oil salesmen and used car lots.

Ditch the elevator pitch. Replace it with your *positioning* statement. The intent of which is to pique the curiosity of the right people (your VIPs and buyers) and engage them in a productive dialogue.

Consider the two phrases that commonly stop us in our tracks when initially connecting with a new prospect or meeting a potential VIP at a networking event.

1. **"Tell me about your company."**

The typical knee-jerk reaction is to give them exactly what they ask for: a fire hose of information about the company.

2. "What do you do?"

The tempting response is to answer the question literally: "I'm a financial planner."

Unless this VIP is seeking the services of a financial planning organization at this moment, his attention is already out the door.

Both of these responses shut down the conversation rather than open a dialogue. So what's the answer? Put your customer at the heart of your conversation and give your words a little CPR.

Jeff, a regional sales executive, posed the question to me at a networking event: "Jill, what do you do?" Knowing that the response "I'm a sales trainer" would have him flee to the hors d'oeuvres table before I could spell "sold," I responded with one of a handful of positioning statements that I keep in my metaphorical back pocket. A statement that tells Jeff immediately what I do, for whom I do it, and the results we achieve.

"You know, Jeff, I have a very cool life, because I get to shift the way sales teams think so that they sell more."

Jeff was curious. "Shift their thinking. So how do you do that?"

Now I was standing at an important fork in the road.

Path #1 lured me to the fire hose of what we do at sales-SHIFT. Sales labs. Training. Speaking. Leadership coaching. Blah blah blah. Ugly gushing sales trainer.

Path #2 directed me to put the customer at the heart of the conversation. To pivot the request so that I was positioning my answer in the context of Jeff, and placing Jeff in my response.

I took path #2. "Well, Jeff, we do this in a number of ways. It depends on the customer's situation. Let's take your sales organization as an example. What's a challenge that your team faces right now?"

He didn't need to think. "I'd say our biggest struggle is balancing new business development with managing existing clients. The business development gets shortchanged because people are uncomfortable with it. What frustrates them is the lack of response to their e-mails and calls. They feel prospecting is a waste of time."

I now had what I needed to put Jeff at the heart of the conversation.

"Jeff, we see a lot of other sales teams struggle with this. And particularly in service industries like yours. The root problem is often how reps think about prospecting. Let me give you an example..."

Now we had put the conversation into Jeff's world. I was able to position salesSHIFT in the context of his team and to continue in a way that drew Jeff further into a dialogue. What might have morphed into a seller monologue was now an opportunity to engage Jeff in a dialogue centered on what matters most to him. He was not forced into the yawn-provoking role of passive listener. And I was able to say less with greater impact.

On top of which, I was:

- Getting an immediate indication as to whether Jeff was a potential VIP.
- Gaining educated insights about Jeff, his sales team, and his company—all of which would enable me to drip with relevance when we parted company.

Jeff's parting words: "Jill, I'd like to get you in front of my team. My challenge is that all sales development is done through our in-house training division. Let me see what I can do."

I could have left him to go figure this out. But I knew once he got back into his frantic world this would fall off his priority list. I liked Jeff. I wanted to stay on his radar. And I wanted to increase his sense of urgency to talk to his executives about engaging salesSHIFT. Better still, I wanted to create an opportunity to speak directly with his senior team. And so I dripped. Three months later, I delivered my first training lab to his team.

If you are thinking your own positioning statement needs a little resuscitation, here's a great exercise to do as a team. Develop a one-sentence positioning statement that paints a picture of:

C: The **Customers** for whom you do your best work.

P: The **Priority** or **Problem** you address.

R: The **Results** you achieve.

Then create relevant versions of your positioning statement for different client segments. For example, when I am speaking with a small-business owner, I use a modified and relevant adaptation of my positioning statement. Knowing that many members of this audience are uncomfortable with selling, when asked, "What do you do?" I respond with, "I help business owners (Customer) sell confidently and competently (Priority) so they grow their business faster (Result)."

People may ask, "What do you do?" But, frankly, they don't care what you do. They care about what you can do for them. If you want to open a dialogue, then forget elevators. Put the customer at the heart of your conversation. And give the conversation a little CPR.

Position to win at any price

A RETIRED FRIEND frequently gives me hell because I shop at a very expensive grocery store. I pay $6.99 for lettuce compared to her $1.49. She constantly reminds me it's all the same: green leaves. And she's right.

But here are my circumstances. My life moves at warp speed. When I head home at the end of a busy day I am either fighting gridlocked traffic with other worn-down commuters or struggling to stay alert, having flown in from a speaking gig in another time zone. All I want to do is get home, eat light, and sleep deep.

Three minutes from my house is a quality, albeit high-priced, grocer with an unparalleled butcher and the freshest produce. He sells triple-washed lettuce in a box, which I dump straight into the salad bowl when I land in my kitchen. No time-consuming washing, spinning, chopping. (Yes, this is how I cook. Never accept an invitation to my house for dinner.)

What's important to me? My time. Convenience. I'm prepared to pay almost five times as much for a commodity just to satisfy these two priorities. My friend, on the other hand, does everything to stretch her retirement income as far as possible, even if it means driving fifteen minutes out of her way to save 50 cents on a head of lettuce. She can nag me about my frivolous spending, rationalize the cost savings, and shock me with the health risks of boxed products until I hit retirement. She's wasting her breath. The only thing that will change how I buy is if she shows me how to satisfy *my* priorities at a lower price.

Now I know that you are selling more complex offerings than lettuce, but nobody (that includes you) wants to pay more than necessary for anything. Unless we have a damn good reason to do so.

Similarly, although organizational buyers have a responsibility to their company and shareholders to avoid unnecessary spending, this doesn't mean customers won't willingly pay more, for the right reasons and under the right circumstances. As a professional seller it's your job to understand those reasons and circumstances and to position the attributes of your recommendation so that your price is perceived to be fair.

Bottom line:

YOU own the price issue.

Consider this: Price is not the *reason* for buying... or not buying.

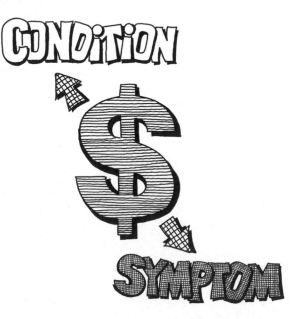

Price is either a condition or a symptom.

Losing the sale on price (and particularly if this comes as a surprise, which it shouldn't) points to one of two issues:

1. Price was a condition of this sale, and you failed to identify this in the discovery process.
2. The price objection is a symptom of you missing a vital piece of information in one or more of the four quadrants during discovery, or a symptom of your failure to *position* yourself to be the relevant choice at a premium price.

What buyers say and what buyers do can be at opposite ends of a spectrum. Don't get stuck in a seller's happy mind-set when you hear the joyful words, "We're not looking for the lowest-cost provider." Understanding whether or not price is a condition has less to do with asking the direct question (although it doesn't hurt) and more to do with listening for clues.

Money, time, and attention flow to priorities. The buyer's willingness to pay a higher rate has little to do with how great your service is and much to do with her perception of the importance of this specific initiative. Early in the discovery process, get clear on the strategic importance of this purchase to the buyer and obtain the customer's perspective on the tangible impact and consequences of making the right or wrong decision. Understand the various stakeholder priorities.

Hélène, a sales manager for a hotel in Eastern Canada, received a call from a company in Finland that had won an important contract in Canada. Oskar was looking for a suitable hotel to house his project team, who would be traveling back and forth from Europe between January and March. The opportunity represented a very attractive piece of business for Hélène—3,000 room nights in the off-season winter months. She crafted a strong proposal, sent it to Oskar, and waited to hear. And then she got the call. The one we've all received at some point in our career. "Hélène, thanks for your proposal. We're in the final stages of making our decision and your competitor's nightly room rate has come in $10 lower than yours. Are you able to sharpen your pencil?" To the client this equated to a $30,000 saving. To Hélène, failure to close this deal represented a potential loss of $300,000 in room revenue. Price had become the deciding factor. Or had it?

Hélène faced a critical decision. It would be easy to do what 90 percent of sales managers in her position would do: offer to talk to her general manager about shaving a few dollars off the rate. But she didn't.

Her response: "Oskar, I understand that you have to do what is right for your group. And before you make your final decision, I want to go back to something you shared earlier. You mentioned that your team wasn't thrilled to be leaving the cold, dark northern climate of Finland to work in an equally harsh winter climate here in Eastern Canada. I want to remind you of our hotel's heated underground parking lot. This means that rather than getting up early to put on their winter gear, walk to a frigid parking lot, unplug the car, scrape ice off the windshield, and then wait in the cold for the car to warm up, your team members simply take the elevator to a warm garage, start the car, and drive immediately to the site, saving them time and discomfort."

Sold.

Hélène may have included "underground parking" as one of many features in her proposal, but his pricing conversation was a symptom of the fact that this important attribute had been missed or forgotten. By reminding Oskar of his words and the interests of his important stakeholders, Hélène was able to reiterate an important connection that won the deal at a premium price. She positioned her hotel so that price was no longer seen as the condition.

Your ability and willingness to hold your price comes from confidence in your earlier exploration of the four quadrants of discovery. If you did a weak job of discovery, it's almost impossible to hold your pricing in the face of cheaper competition or pressure from decision-makers to sharpen your pencil.

Now, if you deduce that price is the #1 condition, common sense prevails. There can be only one lowest-cost provider. In this case, you are now faced with some important questions. Given your competition, can you compete and win? Does your organization want you committing your time and company resources to bid on a losing option? Are you prepared to reduce pricing for this specific win, recognizing that you may have just set a recurring expectation with this client?

If you decide on specific occasions that you are prepared to take on a client who may not have the necessary funding, do this without dropping your credibility. Never devalue your service. Reposition it at the lower rate. That is, if you reduce your price, either remove something from the offer or request something of low cost to the buyer that represents high value to you and your organization. For example, I've negotiated introductions to other qualified buyers, access to expertise, partial contra agreements, and multiyear commitments. Failure to adjust the offer when lowering prices results in you training your customers to pay less and expect ongoing discounts.

The truth about closing

NOWHERE IS THE CONCEPT of positioning more relevant than when it comes to the final step of the sales process. The close.

You work hard to get in front of new customers, and you put extensive time and resources into understanding their issues and perfecting relevant solutions. Given this extraordinary investment, it seems surprising that so many talented salespeople stumble when it comes to moving the customer forward or asking for the business, thus opening the back door to a confident competitor.

I know that many of you are on a relentless search for that one killer tactic that will bring the sales process to a happily-ever-after ending. And I've seen no shortage of closing techniques that range from cheesy to downright manipulative. Take the aptly named "Distraction Close," which suggests that you "catch the client at a weak moment." Or the "Compliment Close": Flatter the prospect into submission by telling her how wonderful she is. Or—drum roll please—the "Selective Deafness Close," which advises you to respond "only to what you want to hear." Yes, these really exist. When studies show that distrust in the sales profession continues to escalate, how can anyone with an IQ higher than that of a goldfish buy into this common nonsense? You can only hope that your competitors are lapping it up.

Here's what you need to know:

Closing "tactics" are redundant.

Closing isn't pushing to make the sale because you want it, or need it, now. Nor is it about spewing a never-ending stream of benefits to force a yes. Closing is positioning the next logical step in the sales process and helping the customer to move forward. That next step may be an agreement to a next meeting. It may be your company's name on the short list recommended to the executive committee. Or it may be signing the contract. If you've explored Q3 (the buying situation), you should know exactly what that next step is long before you seek commitment.

Never lose sight of this: Your ability to move the deal forward with confidence has nothing to do with self-serving "techniques." It has everything to do with how you have positioned yourself throughout the process before the close.

If you are one of the many salespeople who lacks the confidence to ask for that important next step in the sales process, here are some loaded questions. Have you focused on the right input, thus earning the *right* to ask for the commitment of the buyer? Have you consistently contributed relevant value? Have you exercised your curiosity muscle to deeply understand the customer's situation *from their perspective*? Have you clearly connected specific attributes of your recommendation to what *they* deem most important? Are you positioned to be the obvious choice?

If you can confidently answer yes to these questions, the close is as simple as this:

- Ask for feedback on your submission: "So what do you think?"
- Listen to their words and be prepared to dive deep to know whether or not you have nailed their goals, priorities, and interests.
- Address any questions or concerns: "Is there anything we need to discuss before moving forward?"

- Recommend the next step and ask for the commitment: "Hans, if you like what you see, are you ready to put our recommendation in front of your board?"

And if you're thinking, "But Jill, I don't always get an opportunity to have this conversation because I don't physically present the proposal in person," then preschedule a meeting or call to discuss your recommendation *before* final decision-making. Position this step early on as a standard within your proposal submission process: "Our commitment to each customer is to provide a proprietary proposal designed to address your specific needs. In return we ask for your commitment to a brief proposal review before you make your final decision." It's a professional courtesy given the time, resources, and intellectual property you are investing in this customer. Will 100 percent agree to this? No. And that may be your first red flag. But if you don't ask, you're guaranteed a no.

Position everything everywhere

POSITIONING STARTS FROM your very first conversation with a potential new customer. Positioning applies not only to your offering; it applies to your organization. It applies to your role. It applies to you.

New to her company, Eleanor had been assigned a territory. She was struggling. "I don't want potential clients to know that I'm new. It's not good for my credibility. But I don't have much experience with the company, so I don't have a portfolio of client successes to share."

Eleanor needed to shift her thinking. She was focused on trying to hide her newness. She wasn't thinking about how to *position* it. "So, Eleanor," I asked her, "when you were looking to move on in your sales career, did you have choices in a potential employer?"

"Yes."

"So why did you choose to work for this company?"

By the time we finished talking this through, Eleanor had developed an introduction that positioned her recent start at the company as a credibility builder for both her and the company.

"Mr. Prospect, I'm thrilled to be here as your new sales contact for Company Y. I know you have choices when it comes to addressing your organization's technology needs. I was faced with similarly difficult choices when deciding which company to join as the next step in my career.

I thought it might be valuable to share why I am here representing Y. First and foremost I was impressed with the growth of the company. And, more importantly, how its forward-thinking executive team has proactively built and adapted our business model to fully address the shifting needs of our clients. For example..."

Eleanor had now taken the focus off her inexperience. She had put her customer at the heart of the conversation by leading with her understanding that he was faced with a smorgasbord of choice. She was no longer trying to hide her newness under a steady stream of scripted benefits. By leading with the customer and positioning the specifics of her decision to work for this company in a way that highlights relevance and value for the client, she was able to introduce herself with confidence and credibility.

Make the shift

AT 5:00 P.M., following a training class on the topic of positioning, the sales team went home. Except for Don. Based on what he had learned, he returned to his office to rework a proposal due to a client the following day.

How do I know this? Because an e-mail requesting my feedback on his executive summary landed in my inbox at 3:30 a.m. I responded at 8:30 that morning. And by noon the product of Don's all-nighter landed on the client's desk.

Two months later I received an e-mail from Don at a more reasonable hour:

> Jill, we won the business that I wrote the executive summary for the night of our last class with you. Remember the 3:30 a.m. marathon? Anyway, we are currently finalizing the contract terms and pricing, but it looks like approximately $600K to start, with a lot of growth potential.

He went on to share that he believed rewriting the executive summary and proposal to better reflect and connect to his client's perspective, and using the client's words, helped him win this important long-term deal.

So take a page out of Don's proposal. Put this book down now. Pull up a couple of your recent sales presentations, proposals, or messages. Do they simply spew benefits? Or do they follow the LCBS framework to position you to win?

- Do they Lead with the customer's interests, in his language?
- Have you clearly Connected the relevant elements of your recommendation to show *how* you will address the interests of the client's business, stakeholders, and buying process?
- Are you Being specific? Or are you communicating in general platitudes?
- Could you Say less to have more impact?

The more important question: How consistently do you execute this? Positioning is foundational if you want to stand out, differentiate, and win—at any step in the sales process. To keep yourself focused, eliminate verbs like "propose," "present," and "persuade" from your sales vocabulary. Replace them with the word "position."

Listen to the difference. You're not proposing a solution; you are positioning it in the context of my particular situation. You're not presenting your capabilities; you are positioning them according to my needs. Stop writing prospecting messages; create messages that position you as a contributor of relevant value. Do not attempt to persuade me of your expertise; position your expertise in my terms.

Frankly, if you feel like you are pitching, persuading, or convincing me to buy, that's a clue that you've missed something in the sales process. You either neglected to get curious and therefore don't *know* what's important from my point of view, or you failed to *position* yourself in the context of what I care about most. Either way you've just made yourself irrelevant and put the sale in jeopardy.

Only 37 percent of buyers agree that sellers do a good job of tailoring their offering to the customer's needs, proving that many of us need to take a hard look at what we are doing. Ignoring positioning is the express train to failure because it shunts good deals into the hands of inferior competitors. Taking every opportunity to position yourself to be the most relevant will set you apart and, more importantly, skyrocket your close ratio.

Common Nonsense		Uncommon Sense
Pitch	→	Position
Throw in the kitchen sink	→	The discipline of less
Provide a solution	→	Connect the dots
Elevator pitch	→	CPR: Customer, Problem/ Priority, Result
Price is the reason for "no"	→	Price is a condition or a symptom
Closing techniques	→	Be positioned to take the next logical step

6

ROADBLOCKS

Embrace "No"

to Crush Barriers and

Escape Black Holes

HERE'S A LOADED statement: There really are people out there who don't need, or want, what you sell. And not every potential buyer is right for you. Or ready to buy from you *now*. So why continue to act as if they are? And then get disappointed when they aren't?

I met Paul in Miami. He was my dream prospect, the president of a mid-size US-based business, in substantial growth mode. He was smart, well read, and most importantly he shared my belief that people drive the company's success. Just one problem. He made it crystal clear: "Jill, I am not in the market for sales training." He had his own proprietary sales methodology and they were doing fine. It was a no. With the hope of an immediate opportunity off the table, I focused on getting to know Paul, and we parted with a commitment to keep in touch because "situations do change."

Seven months into my drip campaign I received a call from Paul. His exact words: "Jill Harrington, I'm ready. This will probably be the easiest sale of your career. I'll tell you what I want. You'll tell me if you can do it. And, if the answer is yes, we have a deal." No price haggling, no competitors, no time wasted. Sold!

Backtrack to that first conversation in Miami. What if Paul had given me the answer every seller seeks: "Perfect timing, Jill, I am in the market for sales training right now." Fantastic! Actually, no. Remember, prospects who are ready to buy are already well into their decision-making journey. Chances are he is already talking to other sales experts if this is his response. I'd be entering the game late, an unknown at a distinct disadvantage, or just an "additional quote." Getting a no was actually good news. It enabled me to solidify credibility over time through a relevant drip campaign that advantageously positioned me on Paul's radar when the time was right for him.

In this situation I know that getting that initial no helped me win one of my best clients. It provided me space to apply everything we've talked about in this book to increase the odds of a future win at fair rates.

The pressure and desire to find an immediate win causes sellers to view "no" negatively. A disappointment. A failure. It's time to rethink "no." View it is an opportunity to learn and grow. To better position yourself to win. It's common for sellers to blast past no and move on to the next suspect. But there's tremendous value in a no, and in how you leverage it.

"No" comes at different phases of the sales process. It can smack you in the face out of the gate on a first attempt to connect. Or weeks into your drip campaign. It comes in many shades: "I'm ecstatic with my current supplier." "I'm not interested." "Talk to my purchasing manager." "We don't have the budget." "Call me in six months." "You missed the mark." Or the concrete wall of silence.

It can come in the form of a disappointing loss after months of work, allocation of resources, and hours of time developing the "winning" proposal. "We've decided to stick with the status quo." "Your price is too high." "Your competitor provided a better solution." Sometimes a prospect is not looking to buy. Or buy from you. It happens. But don't squander this opportunity to set yourself up for success in the future.

It's uncommon sense. But I want you to consider this: Learn to embrace no. Be prepared to turn an immediate no into a future yes.

Rejection
is cheesecake

I KNOW SOME very capable professionals who are potential sales superstars. But they will not pursue a career in sales because they don't want to face rejection.

So let me scrub this nonsense from your thinking.

Rejection is not part of the smart seller's vocabulary. Rejection is a rightly earned badge of shame of the telemarketer. Take the duct-cleaning services people. They continue to appear on my call display every month as if we're long-lost cousins. Despite my far-from-polite request to "Never, ever call me again!" Despite my officially registering on the "Do Not Call" list and reporting their calls as spam. When I choose to pick up, the conversation always ends abruptly. Either I hang up midway through a scripted self-absorbed monologue, or Mr. Duct Cleaner disconnects when I remind him that he is actually breaking the law. Now that's rejection with a capital R. I am rejecting both product and caller.

But this isn't you.

In the world of professional selling you mustn't confuse rejection with refusal.

Think of it this way.

I *love* cheesecake. I could eat it every day. Seriously. I literally salivate every time I stand in front of the takeout counter at the Cheesecake Factory. The choice!

But there are days when, despite my passion for this 2,000-calorie obsession, I say no. I refuse cheesecake. For one of a number of reasons. I'm trying to squeeze into that little black dress for a high-profile dinner that night, and a cheesecake bump would spoil the whole look. Or I worked out at the gym, ate healthy meals all day, and it just seems wrong to spoil one of those rare righteous days. Or, more likely, I just gorged myself on chocolate, and as much as I'd like to give it a heroic effort, the thought of adding cheesecake to my groaning stomach makes me heave.

The point. I haven't rejected cheesecake. Rejection means "No!"

I have refused it. Refusal means "No, for now."

And so it is with your prospects.

Smart sellers are not rejected. If you've done your homework and provided evidence to suggest there is value in us connecting, here's the truth: You are being refused. A refusal is not personal. It's simply that the time or offering isn't right for me now. Perhaps you've misconstrued the urgency of this opportunity to me. Maybe I'm busy as heck and don't have time to deal with you, or this issue, now.

"No thanks" may be one stakeholder's perspective. I've been refused by a director of human resources on Monday only to be ushered in by his VP of sales on Friday. The speed of change in today's business world and the transient nature of customer "loyalty" means that "no" translates to "no for now."

When you receive a refusal you have a choice. If this is a VIP account, ask yourself, "Is this just one influencer's perspective?" "Is this temporary?" If so, read on to discover how to EARN the right to a future yes. Because you haven't been rejected; you've simply been refused.

EARN the right to yes

I WAS LISTENING in on a call with Gillian. She sells leadership training and development services. When the prospect picked up the phone, his response to her opening message was polite but final. "We've been working with the same company and trainer for the past ten years. We couldn't be happier. I don't need to look at anyone else right now. Thanks."

I've seen this response reduce a smart but ill-prepared seller to a jabbering idiot. There are three common reactions to "We adore our current provider."

1. **"Thanks very much."** Click. The seller disconnects.

2. **A violent attack of verbal diarrhea.** The seller unloads a motherlode of benefits in a mindless attempt to find the one thing that the current cherished supplier is missing. Click. The customer disconnects.

3. **The delivery of one of the many cheese-laden lines circling the internet.** For example, "Have you considered what your loyalty may be costing you?" "I'd like to provide a quote on a next opportunity." "I'm confident that my company and I will earn your business." Click.

Gillian went with a fourth approach. "John, that's disappointing for me. And I understand. We have a number of loyal customers like you. I guess this is the kind of response we hope our customers give. It's not often I get a live response to my calls, so before I go, may I ask you one question? You're a seasoned executive. I'm curious. What specific qualities are important to you in selecting a training provider?"

And John started to talk, taking the conversation deeper into the subject of leadership challenges, trends, and frustrations.

After several minutes John closed the call. "You know, Gillian, it might be smart to have you keep in touch. Something may change." Gillian had turned the brick wall of no into a potential path to yes by using a smart framework. She EARNed the right to move the sales process forward.

E: Empathy

Gillian kicked off her shoes and stepped into the customer's. She acknowledged John's words. "That's disappointing for me. And I understand. We have a number of loyal customers like you." She chose not to justify, defend, or retreat.

She was empathetic to his situation and authentic about her own. By acknowledging his perspective and accepting it (rather than denying it or fighting it), she eliminated the tension between a buyer who wants to end the call and the seller who wants more time.

A: Ask

Gillian avoided the traditional seller-focused question, "May I ask, what do you like about your current training partner?" When I receive this question I see red. My response, "That's none of your business!" I know a lot of buyers will share. But by asking them to gush about your competitor, aren't you reinforcing their adoration?

Before Gillian disconnected she asked a single big open-ended *opinion* question: "What specific qualities are important to you in selecting a training provider?"

The wording of Gillian's question worked on multiple levels:

- It was not a traditional manipulative question centered on making a sale.
- It came from a place of genuine curiosity: her desire to learn.
- People respond favorably when asked for their expert perspective on a subject.
- Asking engages. Telling disengages.

R: Retreat

Gillian did not overstay her welcome. Neither should you. Gillian made it clear to John that she was going to leave: "Before I go..." And because she took a courteous, empathetic approach, he was actually willing to give her more time. But she didn't abuse it. She left this prospect wanting more.

N: Next step

In Gillian's situation the prospect recommended the next action. This won't always happen. Thank the buyer for his input; suggest you stay in touch on whatever time frame you both agree to. Make the commitment to connect only if you have something of relevance to share. Ask for the prospect's preferred method of communication.

Then get the heck off the phone!

By being prepared to step into the EARN framework, Gillian moved the sales process forward in three important ways.

1. She started the process of establishing credibility by distinguishing her response from the myriad sellers who abdicate common sense to a self-serving script or push for an immediate yes.
2. She obtained valuable information *in the buyer's words* that will enable her to initiate a relevant drip campaign.
3. She has the buyer's blessing to continue to be in touch.

Selling is a process. Don't let a refusal stop you in your tracks. When using the phone, be prepared for all possible responses. Have a handful of questions prepared that respectfully ask for the customer's perspective and choose which to use according to the situation, the specifics of why you are calling, and what you are hearing. Engaging the prospect in this type of conversation gets you buy-in and vital information to persist in ways that are relevant to your prospect. Or leads you to the realization that you may be better served diverting your attention to other VIPs.

The EARN framework is a comfortable way to address many other negative responses.

"We may be ready to talk in six months. Call me then."

"Send me something."

"We're really not interested right now."

"We have no budget for this."

Try this: In a sales meeting or with a peer, identify the negative responses you hear most often and brainstorm how you will use the EARN framework to move you forward when others get shut down.

The enemy is your ally

SHOOTING YOURSELF in the foot is both stupid and painful. Agreed? And yet sellers pull the trigger every day. Because they perceive gatekeepers, including purchasing departments and RFPs, as the enemies of sales. No question each of these adds a dollop of complexity mixed with a heap of frustration to the sales process. Even the commonly used term "gatekeeper" encourages the mind-set of having to beat the enemy, or maneuver around an obstacle that is hampering the seller's success.

The purpose of each of these perceived barriers is twofold:

1. To filter out irrelevant time-wasters.
2. To filter in valuable resources.

Common nonsense has sellers operating from the belief that the only mandate of a gatekeeper is #1, which leads to much effort wasted on figuring out a way around "the enemy." The uncommon sense is to align with #2. Focus your opening message on why you fall into the category of valuable resource and position yourself as relevant to the buyer. And her organization. With the right mind-set, you can shift gatekeepers from perceived foes to valuable allies.

Before investing considerable funding into the development and launch of a new service, one of my clients wanted to test its viability with potential buyers. Because of the strategic nature of the service, they needed the input of executives—CEOs, COOs, CFOs, and senior purchasing executives.

Bill hired me to help. He needed someone who understood his business and who had the credibility and ability to garner time and insights from an audience that was tough to engage. I was able to schedule meaningful conversations with almost all of the executives on my list. And I would not have succeeded without the help of the gatekeepers.

If you want to connect with senior executive George, and you know the odds are you'll get his assistant, Carol, prepare your opening message as if you will be talking to George. Use the LCBS framework to lead with what you know is important to George and connect your relevant value. Carol knows what's top priority for George, and she knows and probably controls George's schedule.

And when Carol (or her voice mail) answers, show delight. Not disappointment. Solicit her help. "Carol, I'm so glad I got you. I'm hoping you might be able to help me." Share the message you prepared for George. Provide her the evidence that you fall into the category of valuable resource, not time-waster. Explain that you are seeking a brief (meaning low-risk) fifteen minutes on George's agenda for an exploratory conversation. And that you understand Carol is the right person to find that appropriate time slot.

The gatekeeper is your ally—provided you show up with a genuine ticket to enter, evidence you have a valid reason to speak with George from George's point of view, and a deep respect for Carol's position.

Purchasing nonsense

IF YOU SELL to large organizations, chances are you are required to work with purchasing and procurement specialists. And I'll bet dealing with them is not on your list of favorite things.

Entire sales teams are frustrated because they are no longer allowed to speak with their familiar warm and fuzzy departmental contacts during the RFP process. They struggle to squeeze their unique service into the rigid boxes of the formal purchasing templates. They are frustrated with the limited opportunity to ask questions. And most see red when their smart discovery questions—and the answers— are shared with a field of hungry rivals. I see a lot of finger pointing on the part of sellers who are quick to exclaim, "Purchasing specialists are inflexible. They care only about price. We aren't selling widgets. They don't understand us."

The reality is, we need to point that finger right back in our own direction. According to the purchasing community we, the sales profession, do a pretty sad job of understanding their world. A few years ago this sent me on a mission to better understand this specific breed of buyer. I interviewed a series of professional purchasing and procurement officers from different industries with one intent: to understand their perspective. It was eye-opening and mind-shifting, and it dispelled much of the common nonsense.

Common nonsense: Purchasing specialists are not interested in building relationships with sellers.

Wrong! They need to be connected to sales pros because it is their job to source options. *They require a different kind of relationship.* They are not interested in the feast of self-serving sellers whose intent is to find a way to beat the system or get an advantage over the competition. Nor will they accept invitations to dinners, tickets to the game, or gifts. Their mandate is to ensure an unbiased purchasing process.

And while their conversations with you during the formal bid process need to be documented and shared to ensure complete transparency, most are open to having a telephone conversation when there is no formal RFP on the table. My own experience confirms that they are willing to help you understand their priorities—when you are not trying to sell them something. While they may prefer poring over a spreadsheet to chatting over a cup of coffee, everyone I interviewed was extraordinarily generous with their time and knowledge because my intent was to understand their mandate and learn how to better support their process.

Common nonsense: Decisions are based solely on price.

Yes, cost can be a predominant criterion in the decision-making process. But not always. The mandate for purchasing is not simply to get the lowest price. *It is to ensure a fair and equitable purchasing process. And to avoid unnecessary spending.*

In the purchase of strategic services and products, for example, buyers are looking for long-term, high-value partnerships, coupled with savings opportunities. From the mouths of purchasing: "Companies that will save us money over the longer term, reduce risk, and provide greater value in the context of our business interests will frequently win over the lowest price. But relatively few demonstrate this in their proposals. It inevitably comes down to price when the seller hasn't done their homework." Did you catch those last two sentences?

Common nonsense: The RFP template prevents us from demonstrating differentiated value.

Let's be clear about the intent of the template. *It is to ensure an open and fair process.* Purchasing professionals can be audited on the process, and there can be severe penalties for any evidence of bias. If a requirement on the form is irrelevant to your situation, contact the purchasing officer to question it. Do not ignore it or substitute it. You may be disqualified for an incomplete submission.

As for the issue of demonstrating differentiated value, here's how the purchasing professionals weigh in on this issue: "We assume the seller is the expert on their business and that they have done their homework to understand our organization. We expect them to add fresh and relevant ideas that provide specific strategic value and save money in the context of the bigger picture. Too many proposals are filled with puffery straight from the selling company's website."

So what's the uncommon sense advice to sellers?

Shift your thinking. View purchasing as a potential ally instead of an enemy to be overcome. Substitute that judgmental mind-set for one of genuine curiosity. Look at how you can contribute to their process, not manipulate or fight it. Aim to make it easy for them to do business with you. Don't fill your response with everything impressive about your company that the purchasing department neither needs nor wants to know. Say less with more impact. Demonstrate how the specific expertise you bring will contribute relevant value to their success.

One of the final comments I took away from my interviews: "As in any profession, there are specialists who are fair and some who aren't. There are RFPs that are well written and others that aren't. Know the difference. If purchasing is not prepared to answer questions about the process, then you have a decision to make. Proceed or not."

Always remember this: The RFP is the tail of the sales cycle. If your initial interaction with purchasing is a required response to an RFP, you are walking into the closing stage of the process. If the document provides sketchy information and you have no opportunity to talk to the sender, then you've just skipped all earlier phases of the sales cycle—the ones that enable you to position yourself to win. What you do before the RFP lands is what sets you up for success. Use this time to do your homework and talk to key stakeholders. And set up an information session with purchasing.

My last word and the greatest example of common nonsense on this subject: There appears to be an onslaught of electronic RFPs put out in some industries. As many as one hundred sellers receive the same limited information, with no opportunity for conversation or questions. I don't know who is more insane. Is it the seller who responds, choosing to throw mud at a blank wall and hoping it sticks? Or the buyer prepared to wade waist-deep through a mire of irrelevant information hoping to make a sound business decision?

Steer clear of the abyss

WE'VE ALL EXPERIENCED THIS. A seemingly enthusiastic buyer agrees to review your proposal or to provide you with more information. But when it's time to deliver on that commitment, you feel like you are calling into the abyss. The only sound you hear is the echo of your own voice.

Almost one-quarter of forecasted sales opportunities result in no go. Meaning nobody wins. The deal simply disappears. These situations are a horrendous waste of our attention, time, and resources. So what's causing you to fall into the infamous black hole?

There are a number of possibilities, the common ones being:

- This initiative is a "nice to do" but not critical to the buying organization's success.
- The customer is simply shopping for ideas and information.
- Company policy dictates that multiple bids are required, but there is no intent to change.
- Internal resources are more than capable of doing the job.

Following the advice in chapter 4, flexing your curiosity muscle up front and fully exploring the four quadrants of discovery will help prevent you floundering in the dark.

But more often than we realize, our own sales approach may be bringing us to the edge of the abyss. Consider Chris's situation.

Chris was looking for help. "Jill, I had a good conversation with a new prospect. He sounded very interested.

I offered to e-mail a preliminary proposal and follow up to discuss. He agreed and so I sent this over to him. That was over a month ago. I've tried multiple times and different ways to reengage with him to get his feedback. But it's like he's disappeared into a black hole. Any suggestions?"

We had just completed a three-day training program on sales process, and I wanted Chris to apply the past three days to his dilemma. I answered his one question with two of my own.

"Chris, where are you in the sales process?"

Easy to answer. He pointed to a wall chart of the process we'd spent three days discussing. "I've positioned a recommendation and I'm hoping to get the commitment to the next step."

"And Chris, where is your customer?"

A moment's thought, and two hundred watts of light flashed on.

"Oh!" He pointed back to the chart. "He's right back here. At the start of the process."

Chris's enthusiasm during the first conversation with this prospect had triggered a race through the sales process. There had been no genuine engagement. No opportunity to establish trust. No dive into the four important quadrants of discovery to qualify the urgency and importance of the need. Just the offer to move the sale forward and close a deal. The wrong ABC had taken hold of Chris. He was in a completely different chapter of the book from his client.

Chris was smart. I didn't need to say anything else. He knew he needed to go back to this buyer with a different message. One that requested permission to take a step back and take time to better understand this customer's situation. And it worked. His approach drew the prospect out of the abyss to share a bigger need that required a very different proposal. Chris prevailed in a competitive bid, earning himself a new client initially worth over half a million dollars.

I had a reverse of this situation happen when I received a call from a sales leader looking for sales training. She had been referred to me and she was seeking a proposal. My response: "Brenda, I'd be thrilled to submit a proposal. Let's schedule a meeting to discuss your situation so that I provide you exactly what your team needs to get to your desired output."

Brenda was apologetic. She didn't have a lot of time. She had money in her budget. It needed to be used prior to year-end to ensure funding for the following year. She needed something fast. All big flashing warning lights. Which I chose to ignore. We settled for a telephone meeting, briefer than I had hoped. As I prepared my proposal all I could hear was a nagging voice in my head saying, "You can't win this, Jill. You of all people should know better." I was at the start of the sales cycle and Brenda was at the end of the buying process. Sure enough, a week after I sent my submission, I received the "Dear Jill" e-mail. "Thanks for your proposal. We're going with another vendor."

I later learned through my network that this training initiative never happened. The company executives reallocated the funds to a more pressing initiative. So we all lost. And Brenda lost her budget for the following year.

Avoid the black hole. There are logical steps in the sales cycle: Access. Engage. Understand. Position. Commit. Retain and grow. The problem is that the pressure of today's market is causing sellers to be out of sync with their buyers, with disastrous results. It's easy to be lured by the immediacy of Always Be Closing and skip the early steps—the ones that identify real opportunity and lead to the win. Recognize where the client is in the buying process. Don't be pressured to race ahead by an aggressive client, making it impossible for you to position yourself to win. Provide the client with a valid reason to step back to join you.

And because today you frequently deal with multiple stakeholders, recognize that what is, in theory, a linear process can turn into a giant pretzel. It happened to me in a meeting with the training department of a large financial institution. I was there to present my recommendation after weeks of meetings. One of the company's executives unexpectedly dropped in. While the purpose of this meeting was for me to position my recommendation, I needed to take a step back to align with this important player. I paused to engage the executive with a short introduction and a recap of the intent of the meeting, the planned agenda, and the desired end game—and to ask what he most wanted to get from his time with us. When I returned to the presentation, I was able to connect key relevant points to my new attendee's interests. Neglecting to step back and bring us in sync might have resulted in an important stakeholder dropping into the black hole, and the sale along with him.

If the sales process stalls, you feel stuck, or you lose the buyer into the abyss—take responsibility for pulling him out.

Ask yourself the three essential questions:

Where am I in the sales process?
Where is my customer?
Are we in sync?

Hit the pause button, step into the customer's shoes, and get aligned. Don't assume silence to mean "not interested." It may just mean you're out of step with one another. Do what's needed to have you both standing on the same firm ground so you can move forward together.

Price is a cop-out

EARLY IN MY SALES CAREER I lost one of my favorite accounts to a competitor. I was devastated. My client shared with me that my competitor had come in at a lower price. I had expected that we would be a little higher, but price had never been a deciding factor and I was confused by the decision. And so I asked Andrew if he would be open to taking twenty minutes to provide further feedback. I assured him that this was not a desperate effort on my part to sway the decision. I had accepted the outcome. The business had been formally awarded to my competitor. I simply wanted to learn from the experience and, yes, because they had been a good customer, I wanted to be in a position to win him back the following year.

He agreed to speak with me.

As we reviewed my proposal, Andrew struggled to demonstrate a meaningful price differential. There was something lurking below the surface of our conversation. While a small part of me didn't want to go deeper, I dove. "Andrew, I'm sensing there was more to this outcome than our fee. Let's set the price difference aside for a moment. What else contributed to this decision?"

His cheeks colored. He shifted uneasily—all evidence of his discomfort. "Jill, it was you."

Ouch!

He explained that my presentation to the decision-making committee missed the mark. Having worked with this company for three years, I had assumed I knew the decision-making process. I didn't. I had neglected to consider the personalities and expectations of two new committee members who, as a result of a recent acquisition, were now high influencers. I assumed that my contacts (leaders in the acquiring organization) had the final say; I was wrong. Complacency also blinded me to the fact that my competitor was an incumbent of the acquired company and, therefore, a considerable threat.

I lost for two reasons, neither of which had anything to do with price:

- I was stuck in my own head. As a result I made fatal assumptions.
- I failed to explore the new "buying situation" (Q3) and the preferences of the two most important stakeholders (Q4).

My competitor had done his homework. He outsold me fair and square.

Buyers are sheepish about their reasons for saying no, and "price" is the easy response because the nice guys don't want to kick you when you're down. Well, I say be willing to take the kick. Give the buyer permission. I had to push Andrew to help me learn from a devastating experience. I told him, "Andrew, don't sugarcoat it!" It was a bitter pill for him to administer and it was still harder for me to swallow. But I'm thankful that I persisted past the "price pretense." I learned two important lessons that day.

1. The unquestionable importance of diving deep into all four quadrants of discovery—no matter how experienced you are or how well you think you know your customer.
2. When rationalizing a lost bid, it's comfortable to lay blame on the broad shoulders of price—both for buyers who want to let the seller down easy, and for sellers looking to abdicate responsibility for the loss.

Take this one to the bank: Never blindly accept or assume that price was the "reason" for losing a sale. Be prepared to push through the discomfort (yours and the client's) to get to the root cause of your miss. As painful as that conversation may be, you will garner critical information about how to shift your approach to ensure more wins in the future.

Know why you lose

WHEN COACHING SOME of my trainees I ask about failed bids. The common response: "I think it came down to price." Or "I think the boss wanted to stay with the current provider." My response is always the same. "You think? Or you know?" There's a world of difference between beliefs and facts.

You can't know if you don't ask. Yet only 23 percent of sales professionals involve the customer in reviews of business they have lost.[1] Most choose to review the loss within the privacy of their own walls, with their own sales team or manager. That's nonsense!

And of the 23 percent of sellers who brave the "Why did we lose?" conversation directly with the customer, I'll bet only a small percentage ever get to the full reason for the loss. Remember, the loss may have nothing to do with your product, service, or solution. It may be a lack of clarity in your presentation, or a failure to clearly connect your offer with the customer's priorities. Maybe the format of your proposal makes it tough for the buyer to find relevant information.

Guide the buyer to fill in the important gaps for you. Get the specifics. For example, "Darla, you spent a lot of time helping us understand your specific priorities. How well did we articulate this understanding in our proposal? How well did we equip you to present to your committee? What could we have done to help you more? Did we adequately address the interest of each of the key stakeholders? How could I have done a better job as your sales rep throughout the process?"

And shut up. Give the client space to think and respond. Let the silence linger so that it gets filled by the customer, not you. As tempting as it is to defend yourself, don't. As painful as it is to hear, accept the feedback. Be curious. Resist the temptation to filter or discount what the buyer is saying. You can decide what to do with it later, whether you share it with the team, act on it, or discard it.

Win or lose, a review should be an integral part of your sales process. Set up the expectation early in the process. In return for receiving a proposal from you, get the client's commitment to a prescheduled meeting to discuss your sub-mission—regardless of the outcome. You'll come away with a much deeper understanding of what in your approach is working, and where you need to make a few winning shifts.

What lurks beneath
the objection

WHEN SOMEONE SAYS YES to you, they say no to the alternatives. Therefore, buying from you means a risk of missing out on something better from someone else. This is why buyers have questions or voice concerns throughout the sales process, especially as it comes down to the final stages. When my head is on the company's chopping block I want to be sure I've minimized any risk of it being the wrong decision.

The ability to better "manage objections" is a sought-after skill in sales circles, and there is no end to the training options available to satisfy this need. But in our haste to manage the customer's concerns, we may be managing ourselves into a poor deal.

Take the most common objection: "We love your proposal but the price tag is too rich."

This usually results in one of two seller responses:

1. "Let me go back to my suppliers (or the boss) and see if we can sharpen the pencil."
2. "Well, Jim, it's actually a very competitive price when you consider the caliber of support resources we're providing and the years of experience we're putting on your project."

The former just shaved dollars off your margin and set a precedent for the future. The latter basically says to your customer, "You're wrong!" Not a smart thing to do at this stage in the sales cycle.

A customer faced with the high stakes of making an important decision wants to get it right. Or at the very least feel confident she has done her due diligence. Underneath every objection, there is something on the customer's mind: a question that needs to be answered or a concern that needs to be removed. I can think of more than twenty reasons why a customer might share this "price tag" objection.

Here are five:

1. **I see the value of your proposal.** But how do I convince my executive to buy in?

2. **You are considerably more costly than the competitor.** Why is that?

3. **There are a lot of components in your recommendation.** Do I need all of them?

4. **Is there a less expensive route to my end goal?**

5. **This is fantastic, but I simply don't have the budget.** Where will I find the money?

Every one of these concerns is outwardly expressed as a price objection. But each one is a distinctly different issue requiring a different resolution. None requires you to drop your price.

Remember the iceberg from chapter 4? When you run into an objection, you've hit another berg. So what do you need to do? Dive deep to discover the hidden 90 percent. Always Be Curious.

Be empathetic, not defensive. Let the customer know that you appreciate this is an important decision and that you want to address her issue. Ask her to share the *specific* concern about the pricing. If you discover that the source of the concern is getting the executive team to agree to a larger investment, you can now address the real challenge. Open a collaborative dialogue that centers on what she needs to confidently position your solution to her executive. And offer support from you and your team.

If she believes that, from an executive perspective, you've overloaded the solution, be prepared to revisit your offer. Use the LCBS framework to Lead with her organization's interests and Connect the value of each component to their priorities. Be specific when speaking to each component and resist the temptation to talk too much. Say less with more impact. You may both agree that there is a place to scale back. Make that informed adjustment before reducing your price.

This principle applies to other objections. "We're not sure that you have the capability to execute this project." "We're concerned about your timelines." "We're concerned about bringing in a new supplier at this time." Before jumping to resolve the wrong issue, the stated concern that sits above the waterline, think ABC: Always Be Curious. Dive deep for the question beneath the objection. Then work with your client to resolve the real issue, and move forward.

A word of caution: Don't assume "We need to think about it" is an objection. If this is an important decision, people need to look at options and want time to process what has been presented. If you've explored the buying situation, this will not be a surprise. Forcing the close is the common nonsense that will push you to the edge of the abyss.

Use the EARN formula to show empathy. You understand it's an important decision. Ask for their perspective on your presentation submission. Ask, and suggest, what you might provide to help them through their thought process. And then retreat with a scheduled next step. While they are thinking about it, be the smart seller who drips relevant value so that you maintain a positive position on the customer's radar throughout their process. Be the safety net that takes the risk out of the buyer's decision.

Have the
courage to say no

I AM IN AWE OF PAT, a small business owner. She made the mammoth decision to fire a high-profile client. A Goliath of a Fortune 500 client. After years of being pitted against inferior competitors and winning the business only to be negotiated further down in price, this modern-day David said, "Enough!" Although having the global brand on her client list added clout to her marketing efforts, she looked at the toll the account was taking on her staff, her suppliers, and her profits. While her competitors fought like cats to get a piece of this company's budget, Pat decided to let hers go.

Sometimes it simply makes sense to say no. Smart sales pros say yes to the *right* opportunities. And they have the courage to say no to those that do not represent good business. For the rest of us mere mortals, it's hard to say no to any lead that lands in front of us. It's like saying no to buying a lottery ticket when the jackpot hits twenty million dollars. We understand that the odds of winning are a hair above zero. But you just never know.

There are circumstances when anything or anyone that shows interest in your company looks good. Right? You're new to the job, market conditions are horrible, you just lost a big opportunity... Wrong! Every time you kiss a frog, you delay finding that prince. Every minute you spend on a proposal you won't win is focus you've taken away from one you could have won.

So when does it make sense for you to say no?

THE OPPORTUNITY IS NOT WINNABLE

You are simply not the right fit. The trouble is, when we're out there seeking the next big win, we often can't see or hear the obvious. I was referred to a technology company by one of my students. Whenever possible, I want to find a way to win a referred piece of business, but in this case as I listened to the executive of this company share his situation, I knew that this company's needs did not match either my focus or my strengths. I could have made it work, but only at the risk of falling short of expectations and at a huge cost in attention, time, and resources. I respectfully declined, recommended a couple of sales development organizations that I believed would hit their sweet spot, and kept the door open by offering my support and expertise if they needed an objective sounding board.

THE PROSPECT IS ON A SHOPPING EXPEDITION

The customer wants a proposal or quote but doesn't have time to provide you with the information you need to deliver a winning recommendation. Seller beware! This prospect is either a "shopper" or the issue isn't important enough for him to devote time and energy to getting it right. And if it's not that important to the customer, there's a likelihood of two outcomes: It either falls into the abyss of "nobody wins," or it comes down to price. You'll work hard and give away your expertise and time with little likelihood of a positive outcome.

THE CUSTOMER IS A "RESOURCE SUCKER"

Just like Pat, most of us have encountered one of these: a "big fish" that's appealing to us for so many reasons. High revenue. Recurring business. A prestigious name on our client list. There's just one problem. Once you reel it in, you can't make a profit on it. The client is ultra-demanding, she wants everything for nothing, and your best employees are stretched to their limit. And even though you blow her expectations out of the water, she puts the contract out to bid every year so you never get paid a fair price for your superior results.

THE CUSTOMER WANTS TO "PAY YOU LATER"

He loves your proposal, he wants to work with you, but he's not prepared to make an up-front financial commitment. Your company is *not* your new customer's bank. If he's given you the green light, and you've made the commitment to allocate resources and start work on his behalf, then he needs to ante up. I've seen many sellers, particularly in the service industries, give away their ideas, their time, and their services without any kind of financial commitment from their customer. This is simply bad business practice.

Walking away can be the right thing to do. But am I suggesting you say no to any opportunity that falls short of the perfect sale? Absolutely not! There are a number of reasons why it may make sound business sense to say yes to seemingly marginal opportunities; for instance, strategic reasons (to get a foot in the door with a new high-potential account), political reasons (your European office is doing big business with this client), or personal reasons (it's an industry you want to support).

Here's what I am saying: Be deliberate and thoughtful in the choices you make. Decide where to focus your attention. Say no to the energy burners that will lead to nowhere. And say yes to the opportunities that you can, and want to, win.

Make the shift

NO IS A WORD that salespeople generally abhor. When it comes from the mouth of a prospect, it signals bad news. And when we use it, it means turning down a potential future win—something that goes against our reason for being.

My key message to you is this: Don't let "no" scare you. Shifting to a mind-set of "embrace no" under the right circumstances is the uncommon sense that enables you to be smarter about choosing the customers that are right for you. And it will prevent you from prematurely quitting on the one that will one day rank at the pinnacle of your client list.

Common Nonsense		Uncommon Sense
Fear rejection	→	Embrace refusal, "No for now"
Fight a no	→	EARN a yes
Avoid the gatekeeper	→	Understand your allies
Follow the sales cycle	→	Align with the buy cycle
It always comes down to price	→	Price is a cop-out
Manage the objection	→	Address the concern beneath the objection
All business is good	→	Have the courage to say no

7

RETAIN AND GROW

Avoid the Shark Pool

I HAVE USED the same phone company since I launched my business in 2002. Despite frequent jaw-dropping incentives from the other ones, I've never strayed. In the eyes of my current provider, I am a loyal customer. But nothing could be further from the truth. If anyone were to ask me to recommend this company, my response, depending on the day, would range from being downright negative to offering an apathetic "They're fine. For a phone company."

I'm satisfied with them when all is running well. But when I hit a technical snag, a billing error, or any kind of dissatisfaction that requires me to call into their customer service center, my perspective shifts. Occasionally I get a rep who defines the words "customer service." More often, I'm growing old waiting to speak to a human being who may or may not be willing or able to do much of real value.

So if I feel this way—and I know many of you are nodding in agreement—why don't I switch phone companies?

The "F" word of course. Fear. Fear that the promise of a seamless transition to the "other guys" won't pan out and that my business will be interrupted. Fear that the devil you know is actually as good as it gets. Fear that the promise of perfect service and cost savings will disappear abruptly once the twelve-month honeymoon period is over. So why go through the hassle? Fear leads to this kind of stultifying apathy and willingness to settle for mediocrity.

Having said this, it would simply take one smart competitor to invest a modicum of effort into understanding my interests and current disgruntlement and then thoughtfully position their offering, shift my perspective, and eliminate my fear. And, finally, deliver on their promise.

Salespeople work hard to bring new customers on board. But customer devotion can be shallow and fleeting. Like me, your customers may be a school of vulnerable fish swimming in a shark-infested pool: potential prospects for a hungry competitor. When you apply a little uncommon sense, you keep your best fish out of the jaws of others so that they become the growth engine for your future sales.

Why you don't
want customers

COMPANY EXECUTIVES and salespeople frequently misinterpret customer behavior. They mistake habit for loyalty. They believe satisfaction creates a life-long raving fan. But that's quite a leap. Think of it more like this: Satisfaction is like a date; loyalty is the marriage. And not all dates lead to marriage.

Charles is the president of a financial services organization and is proud of his company's 90 percent client loyalty factor, meaning that 90 percent of his customers continue to do business with his company every year. Impressive. Until I drew a picture of the customer satisfaction scale and asked him, "Where does this 90 percent sit? How many are advocates? How many are with you out of habit, fear of leaving, or inertia?"

I wasn't trying to burst his bubble. His statement had simply got me thinking about the definition of "customer loyalty." "Long-term" and "repeat" are not synonymous with loyalty.

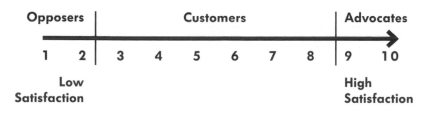

Like my phone company, you have customers across the satisfaction scale. And, like me, many of those customers will fluctuate up and down the scale depending on the situation and how your company meets specific expectations and delivers results.

Thankfully, most of us have few, if any, opposers. These are the customers who are never satisfied but continue to do business with you. Some will eventually leave. Some won't. Those who stay will privately and publicly complain and potentially sour others' opinions of you, using word of mouth, online reviews, and social media to spread their dissatisfaction widely.

Moving up to the middle of the scale, you have customers at varying degrees of satisfaction. Not dissatisfied. But not leaping out of their socks. They don't complain, they keep coming back, and so we assume that they are loyal. Simply put, these customers are the vulnerable fish susceptible to the approach of a savvy shark. Maybe a competitor who gets curious about their unfulfilled needs and perceived switching costs, and then uses this information to position his company to be a more relevant provider. When this happens, the customer leaves. Often silently, without notice, and through the back door.

Vulnerability diminishes as you move to the far right of the scale. Here sit your advocates. These customers derive so much value from your contribution that they publicly support and recommend you.

You want advocates. And you want an army of them because advocates help you advance sales:

- Advocates refer you to others both inside and outside of their own organization.
- They are a source of testimonials that build credibility in your sales messages.
- Advocates buy more and pay more.

- They are willing to give you time, tell you the truth, and share information that keeps you ahead of the sharks.
- Advocates forgive your boo-boos, provided you take responsibility and minimize the pain.

Advocates are loyal.

Loyalty trumps habit. Never confuse the two. If you've simply become a habit to your customers, someone will willingly come in to help them break the habit. Loyalty is a valuable asset that you can leverage to grow your business with greater ease and speed.

Here's my point. Do *not* settle for customers. Cultivate advocates. Failure to do this puts you at risk.

Consider the three questions I asked Charles:

1. Realistically, where are your customers on the satisfaction scale?
2. What do you need to do to move more of your customers up the satisfaction scale to join the ranks of other advocates?
3. How do you currently leverage your existing advocates to identify and connect with qualified new buyers?

Want some help with this? Read on.

When results
don't matter

GABRIELA WAS PUMPED. The account executive for an audio-visual production company, she had just outsold a longtime incumbent to win an opportunity with a large pharmaceutical company, producing their annual state-of-the-nation event. It was the biggest event of their year, and thousands of employees from different areas of the company would attend. This year was special, a milestone anniversary, and the marketing director responsible for the event wanted fresh ideas. The creativity demonstrated by Gabriela's team, coupled with their credentials, had tipped the balance. She won the bid. The client had entrusted her team with all aspects of the event—from staging, lighting, and décor through speech editing, and coaching the executive team. If this went well, Gabriela could have a very big future with this new client.

The big day came. The special effects, light show, and visual presentations left the audience shouting for more. Operationally it was seamless. Energized by this high-wattage success, Gabriela and her producer came to the post-event debrief meeting prepared to talk about building on this success in the future with this client.

The director of marketing thanked Gabriela for a great day. And then dropped the bomb. "Gabriela, I'm sorry. We will not be renewing your contract for next year." Gabriela felt her insides curl. "There's no question you put on the show of a lifetime. One of the best, from our employees' perspective. Thank you for that. But the process of getting there was unacceptable to our leadership team. And they were more than disappointed when you came in over your original estimate. We respect that you incurred overtime costs due to the availability of our executives and the late submission of their presentation scripts, but we explained at the outset that we were paying you to manage this. You put our executives under unnecessary pressure with the push to meet last-minute deadlines. They refuse to work this way in the future. The decision is final."

No second chance. The relationship was over.

A successful output is no guarantee of future business. The process of getting there is equally important. Of course results matter, but a strong output does not necessarily create advocates.

Think of it this way. You are driving for hours through mountainous wilderness to view what you understand to be the most spectacular sunset. If the journey takes you through jaw-dropping scenery and provides glimpses of unusual wildlife and photo opportunities along the route, chances are you'll recommend the drive to your friends. But if the drive requires hours of treacherous roads with little to see along the route and you arrive in time for a mere fifteen minutes of brilliant color, you probably won't be talking up the trip to your pals.

And if you're thinking that as a salesperson the implementation is out of your control—"My operations and service teams are responsible for this"—think again. The journey starts with the client's first interaction with you. It travels through the entire sales process right up to the end result. Salespeople play a critical role in creating an army of advocates, and it all starts with understanding expectations.

It's all about expectations

I LOVE CARS. When I was younger I drove Toyotas. Great brand. Reliable. Affordable. I used my local dealership for servicing. I was happy. The service team was helpful, not pushy, and I never felt that I was being oversold. And when they needed to keep my Celica for an extended period, they provided me with a loaner, something I had not expected.

Then I bought my first luxury set of wheels.

I had seen the car of my dreams on the streets of New York City and knew immediately that this would be my next vehicle. A hot-looking convertible, copper brown, black ragtop, standard transmission. Fully upgraded. And not a Toyota.

My local dealer had the car on the lot, but in white. I did not want white. I could have ordered the car to my exact specifications and waited for it, but having just returned from living in New York I was in a hurry to acquire a new set of wheels. When I asked the salesman to check other dealerships in the area he quickly confirmed the car could not be found in the Toronto area. Not satisfied, I did some research myself, and found my copper-brown baby in a city center showroom less than twenty-five miles away. I felt a mix of anger and disappointment. My baseline expectations of this brand were honesty and a willingness to try harder.

I loved that car from the minute I drove it off the downtown lot. But I handed it back three years later. I hated owning it, servicing it, the condescending attitude at every visit. No loaner was provided. No call or apology for the frequent delays in completing the work. These were baseline expectations that had been satisfied by a less expensive brand. From a luxury car company I expected more. A helluva lot more!

Customer satisfaction and dissatisfaction have nothing to do with how great a job you do. Or don't do. It has everything to do with the job you do *in the context of each customer's individual expectations.*

As a salesperson, your perspective of how well you are executing on the job is irrelevant. You cannot operate under the mantra of "treat people how you want to be treated." That's crazy thinking. It has no relevance in sales. Treat each unique customer the way he or she expects to be treated. Don't make one customer's expectations a universal truth for all clients. And if you don't have an accurate understanding of what each client expects, then it's your job to find out. The customer sets the bar—and it's a moving bar. Your customer's expectations will change over time, so you need to stay tuned in to them throughout the relationship.

One of the smartest, yet uncommon, steps in the sales process is to schedule a conversation to discuss expectations whenever you close a new piece of business. "Noah, we want to thank you for this opportunity. And in order for us to ensure you are delighted with your decision to move forward, we want to talk about what's important to you as we move into implementation. And to share what we will need from your organization to deliver your desired results."

I interviewed Jean as part of my research into the luxury hotel market. She buys conference space for a large non-profit association. Jean was candid. "Honestly, Jill, at the luxury level they're all pretty much the same. The hotels all offer impeccable service, they're beautiful, and the facilities first-class. Most of them are in prime locations within their city. Even their rates are comparable.

"But let me tell you why I choose, again and again, one company over the others. We require very specific terms in our contracts. Reviewing and negotiating individual hotel contracts to make sure they meet our requirements is a big drain on my time. And it's a money suck in legal fees.

"There is a national sales rep with one company who has made it her mission to understand this. She is like the computer chip inside my head. She understands what we need and why we expect specific terms. She will not forward any proposal to me until her hotel has incorporated the concessions and terms that meet our requirements. She does this consistently, and she saves me so much time, money, and frustration that I give her company first option."

When it comes to delivering on our clients' expectations, we can all get it right some of the time. And anyone can blow the customer's expectations in the honeymoon period of a new client relationship.

I know that my luxury car experience is not indicative of every dealer. I have friends who rave about the brand that was my biggest disappointment. And I'm sure if I had stuck with them I might have, at times, experienced the extraordinary service for which they are renowned. But that's not good enough.

A consistently positive experience of working together drives customer loyalty. And a *consistently* good experience *over the long term* cultivates advocates.

> Consistency is the differentiator
> that shifts a customer to an advocate.

Once you start this conversation with your customer, you've set the bar high. Don't encourage your customer to share their expectations unless you plan to act on them. Promising to deliver is only the bottom of a steep climb. And if you trip up on the follow-through, it can be a painful fall.

The sale is not the finish line

BARRY WAS DUMBFOUNDED when his client told him that he had just concluded an extensive bid process to source outside marketing expertise. Barry had been working with this client for years.

"Tyrone, how come you didn't include us on the bid?"

Tyrone's response, "You guys don't do marketing campaigns."

"Sure we do. We added a full marketing arm a year ago."

It was news to Tyrone.

Just like in an Olympic sprint, the close is not the time to slow down. You work hard to bring on new customers. Now that you've got them, you want to keep them. And you want to leverage and build on the relationship you've painstakingly forged. Advocates are created by ruthlessly and continuously executing the triad of selling ABCs throughout the life of the relationship. Don't neglect them once you've made the sale.

Had Barry thought to be more *curious* about this customer's business, had he observed and listened for clues to contribute greater value, had he thought to *connect* his company's new offering to this long-term client's success, had he been more present... Then he might have identified a new way to *contribute* to this company's success and been the proud owner of a larger contract, a deeper relationship, and a powerful advocate for his company's new marketing division.

Common sense, right? Yet "over 60 percent of sales organizations report dissatisfaction with their ability to cross-sell and upsell."[1] Given that most salespeople are more comfortable talking to existing customers than initiating conversations with new prospects, this statistic reeks of common nonsense.

Busyness, complacency, and the assumption that "no news" translates to "all is good with the status quo" are major obstacles that stop salespeople from transforming customers to advocates. Perhaps this silence is the quiet sliding of your new relationship backward through the satisfaction scale into the shark pool.

Avoid Barry's disappointment.

In addition to continuously executing your selling ABCs and following your client organizations in both online and offline media, schedule periodic "no-selling" conversations with important stakeholders. These conversations have one purpose: to understand the evolving thinking, working, and priorities of the company and stakeholders so that you can proactively bring ideas that contribute to their success. You'll deepen your understanding of other key stakeholders within the organization. You'll get a sense of who you need to know—and who needs to know you. Your input is genuine interest in your client and their business. The output is almost always information that will enable you to contribute in ways that will strengthen the relationship, grow the account, and keep this treasured client away from the sharks.

Similarly, salespeople play an important and proactive role in obtaining feedback.

When a regional sales executive proudly shared his team's consistent rating of ten out of a potential ten on the company's client survey, I was impressed. And curious. "So what's driving that number, Tom?" Red-faced, he shared that no one had dug deeper into this impressive stat.

The team was just happy to receive the ten. But if the ugly number three were to show up on the survey, "We'd be all over it. To figure out the cause of this customer's dissatisfaction," says Tom.

Receiving such lofty scores is valueless unless you understand what's driving them. Getting the specific reasons for these top marks directly from the customer provides you with meaningful testimonials. More importantly, it tells you and the company exactly what you need to do more of to create more advocates.

Get curious. Pick up the phone. Thank clients for their input. "John, we appreciate the recognition. And because we want to continue to do great work for you, we'd appreciate hearing what prompted you to give us top marks so that we can pass this on to the team." Get the specifics. Better still, find out what could take you to an eleven. Without feedback it is impossible to cultivate advocates for your product, service, or organization.

If you're serious about converting customers into advocates for you and your organization, ask these two simple questions throughout the life cycle of the relationship:

- "How are we doing?" Find out how the company is doing, in terms of the customer's expectations.
- "How am I doing?" Find out how you, the sales rep, are doing in the context of your client's expectations.

Schedule these "relationship meetings" on a periodic basis. And remember your role is twofold: to ask these two questions, and to *listen* to your customer's response.

Give your customers a reason (you want to do good work for them) and permission (you're looking for candid feedback) to provide you with sincere, detailed input. Use these meetings to understand what you currently do well. (Keep doing.) What you don't. (Stop doing.) And how you might improve. (Start doing.)

Be open to receiving constructive input. If the customer's perspective doesn't mesh with your own, avoid the knee-jerk reaction of defending your position or pointing fingers to reasons outside of your control. If you filter what you hear through your seller's mind-set, you defeat the entire purpose of asking for the customer's perspective. And if the customer doesn't feel heard, he'll be reluctant to share in the future.

Neglecting to check in with your customers regularly may gradually lead them to think that perhaps you aren't working hard enough to keep their business. I guarantee your competitors are asking your customers questions about how you are doing. The sharks are looking for any morsel to win over a buyer who may not be completely satisfied or who may be led to feel that you don't fully value their relationship.

We've all heard how much harder it is to bring on a new client than to grow business from an existing customer. Work closely with your current clients to create advocates. All it takes is a genuine desire to learn and a ruthless commitment to your new selling ABCs.

Be the
eyes and ears of
your company

I MENTIONED I love cars. And the thrill of owning a new one. But I hate the process of buying one. In fact, I don't know many people who enjoy it. It's a little like your annual physical: You know exactly what is going to happen. None of it is pleasant. And yet it has to be done. You know what I mean:

You walk in to the car dealership prepared to play the game.

You ask for the best price.

You get an unacceptable response.

You ask for a better price.

You receive an apologetic no.

You prepare to walk to the exit.

You get called back. "Let me talk to my manager and see what we can do."

You wait nervously for the completion of their private charade in a back office.

You eventually head home with a shiny new car ... and an overwhelming desire to take a shower.

Bill owns an Infiniti dealership. He is also a really smart sales guy. I walked into his dealership after visiting multiple others with my expectation of the car purchasing experience well below ground level. I had never driven an Infiniti. I knew nothing about the brand. I had, however, fallen in love with a drop-dead-gorgeous hardtop convertible strategically parked out front to ambush passing motorists like me. After two brief visits to the dealership and a short test drive, I was ready to trade in my Audi.

When the Infiniti sales rep shared that Bill, the owner, would be coming to work out the pricing with me, I was confused. "Did I say something to offend you?" No, apparently this was the norm at Bill's dealership. "Bill prefers to talk pricing directly with our customers. He'll sit with you at the computer and you'll work it out together. He wants you to be happy with your new car purchase."

So Bill sat with me. No games. No pressure. Just a sincere interest in meeting my terms on price and trade-in value. Maybe the month-end had something to do with it. All I knew was that, for the first time, I was enjoying the process of buying my new wheels. And I walked out feeling that I had just got the best deal ever.

When I returned the following week to pick up my new purchase, I was greeted by Bill, the sales rep, and the service manager who enthusiastically shook my hand and let me know that he was looking forward to keeping my new baby in pristine running order. What's more, I believed him.

This experience set a whole new standard for the car-buying process for me. I gushed like a fire hose about this fabulous adventure to friends, family, and complete strangers for months. When I asked Bill why he chooses this time-consuming transparent approach to selling cars, he responded: "I see and hear how people feel about the car purchasing process. It's not good. Buying a car should be a fun experience. And the outcome should feel good. I want my dealership to stand apart from others. Eliminating what is most distasteful for the buyer is helping me do that. And it's generating a steady stream of referrals."

So what does this have to do with you? Salespeople have an important strategic role—one that gets forgotten in the frenzy of Always Be Closing. You are the eyes and ears of your organization, with your customers and within your market. And you're the voice of the customer to your company. Your daily presence on the front line provides the opportunity to notice patterns, as Bill does; to listen for what customers value and what they don't; to hear perceptions about the market, about you, and about your competitors. Bill noticed what car buyers were saying and feeling, and he decided to eliminate the most painful step in the car buying process.

Playing the strategic role of observer in your market enables you to uncover client pressure points, redundancies, and service gaps. Unearth valuable data to take back to your team, your marketing department, and your leadership. You can bring game-changing insights that will help you retain your high-growth clients and convert them into advocates with the potential to further grow your sales.

Put your advocates
on the front line

DISTRUST IN SALES and marketing messages has skyrocketed in recent years. Only 6.7 percent of buyers find information provided by sales extremely trustworthy.[2] That's shocking. But sadly, it's not surprising when you see some of the common nonsense and ridiculous unsubstantiated claims made by unthinking salespeople.

Although many skeptical buyers no longer believe the words of sales and marketing, most will believe the words of your customers. This is why legitimate client testimonials and referrals are a powerful sales tool.

Every salesperson loves to receive endorsements from clients. They frequently open doors to new business. But not all of your raving fans provide them. Why not? Because you don't ask! While statistics suggest that almost all customers say they would be willing to provide referrals to their best vendors, very few salespeople are willing to ask for them.

Why don't more sellers proactively ask for referrals and testimonials? Some of the answers I've heard: "Because it's self-serving and pushy." "It feels uncomfortable." "It reeks of desperation."

If you've spent five minutes with a customer and are pressing for a rave review before they've had any kind of meaningful experience with you, or if you're one of those annoying connections who asks someone you've never worked with to post a recommendation on your LinkedIn profile—yes, that comes across as pushy. But if you ask the right people (your advocates) at the right time, it's a natural progression of the conversation. And most advocates are delighted to oblige.

There is no better time to ask for an endorsement than when you've earned the right. When your customer is praising your company's work. So *create* opportunities for them to do this. Schedule a debrief meeting at the end of an important project. Or use a relationship meeting to request input. Or simply invite them out to lunch or dinner.

If the customer is extolling their delight with you, your service, your company, thank them and ask if you may use their words in your sales and marketing. Offer to send their comments in writing for their approval. Don't let this excellent opportunity to obtain a glowing testimonial pass you by.

As for turning your client's praise into a referral request, simply continue the conversation: "Thank you. We're really enjoying working with your team. In fact, as we continue to grow our business we'd like to find more clients just like you. Perhaps you know of someone inside or outside of your organization who would benefit from our services. We do our best work for companies that . . ." And share your VIP profile.

BEYOND BEING A gold mine for glowing testimonials and referrals, your very best customers can actually help you do your job more efficiently and with less frustration. Salespeople have a lot of unanswered questions and often look to sales experts, colleagues, or even strangers online for answers. And we all know that a lot of the advice being freely offered in various sales chat groups is questionable.

The big hairy questions I know sellers desperately want answered include:

- How do I get in front of my ideal prospects faster?
- How do I get them to pay my price?

- What types of messages get their attention?
- What separates us from others in our field?
- Who else would benefit from my services?

You know who has the credible answers to these questions? Your best customers. The customers you'd like to clone. The customers who love you, respect the work you do, and are eager to support your success. Your advocates.

They know exactly what it takes to get the attention of other prospects just like them.

They know exactly why they pay your premium price. They know why they originally bought from you and why they continue to buy from you. They know others who will appreciate the same quality of service.

So when did you last seek their help to get your important questions answered?

Converting customers to advocates is an important step in not only retaining, but also expanding, business. That's uncommon sense. But craziness kicks into top gear when sellers fail to leverage these uber-customers once they have them. Neglecting to provide them with an opportunity to help you grow is a tragic waste of one of your most valuable sales resources. Remember, these raving fans are the very people who want to see you succeed. All you have to do is ask.

Not all referrals are golden

THERE IS NO QUESTION that referrals open new doors, often with less effort than other methods of prospecting. However, referrals are not golden in and of themselves. The likelihood of you actually winning good profitable business from a referral depends on:

1. The quality of the referral.
2. How you ask for it.
3. How you use it.

Are you getting referrals that are winnable and desirable for your organization? I've received some that are not. And once the introduction is made, it can be awkward to pull back. So let your referrers know what type of opportunity represents good business for you. Share your VIP profile, and the type of work at which your company excels.

Just as curiosity helps you uncover priceless information from a prospect, so will being curious about a referral help you increase the likelihood of it being a worthwhile investment of your time. If I suggest you speak to Gregg Smith at XYZ Company, do *not* go with the common nonsense of asking for an introduction. Well, not yet. Instead, get curious. Thank me for the referral and ask why I believe Gregg would benefit from your call.

If it is a legitimate referral, I will have specific evidence for why Gregg will welcome you in. "Well, Gregg shared that his association is struggling to attract new members, particularly from the younger demographic that will fuel future growth. He wants to develop a stronger social media strategy for his organization. Sounds like he's received a lot of poor advice. You really helped us improve our digital presence; maybe you could do the same for him."

Now you have compelling evidence. Rather than calling Gregg and saying, "Jill suggested we talk," (bland) or relying on me to get you access (you've just given up control of the sales process), use the LCBS framework to position the evidence I provided.

"Gregg, Jill Harrington suggested there'd be mutual benefit in you and me connecting. She mentioned you're looking to fuel membership growth from a younger demographic. Jill hired us a year ago to pump up her digital presence for the very same reason. She's been thrilled with the resulting increase in web traffic and leads to her company. Sounds like it's worth a twenty-minute introductory call to see if we might also help you get the right social strategy in place."

Be sure to get to the heart of a referral so that you can identify whether this is a prince or a frog, and so that you have evidence you can use to position yourself with this potential VIP.

Think of testimonials in a similar way—as mini-referrals working on your behalf to win new business. Unfortunately, many sales professionals fail to use their clients' praise to its full potential in their sales messages, proposals, presentations, and conversations. The use of *relevant* testimonials has helped me and my clients access new contacts faster and close more deals.

The trouble is, too many websites and proposals are filled with what I call "smiles," claims of "Awesome job!" "Fantastic work," "I highly recommend XYZ company,"

"Outstanding experience!" These testimonials may make us smile, but they are meaningless.

When you receive or solicit client testimonials, aim for *impact* testimonials, not smiles.

For example, if your customer provides feedback, "You guys were amazing. It's been the best experience ever working with you," don't simply accept the smile. Dive deep to obtain the full impact. You might explore further by saying, "Thank you. We've thoroughly enjoyed working with you. And we want to continue doing great work for clients like you. I'm curious—and I know my team will want to know—what specifically made this the best experience for you?"

Now the client is prompted to provide the detail: "Your project management process was flawless. Your team was always one step ahead of me. The proactivity of your reporting process provided a level of confidence and comfort I've not experienced before. I never once worried about missing a deadline or going over budget."

Now that's an *impact* testimonial worthy of getting in writing. And it's even better if you are able to obtain quantifiable metrics.

I post my clients' words in the usual places—website, LinkedIn profile, tweets, marketing materials, invitations, presentations, proposals—and I use them shamelessly in my prospecting messages to accelerate my drip campaigns. They're a key component of my access arsenal. In my message I'll lead with what I know to be of interest to the prospect and then say less with more impact by using my customer's words to connect our value to their need.

For example, the impact testimonial above would be a very relevant inclusion in an e-mail to a contact who requires tight budget management or has been burned by this issue in the past.

Let your customers' words sell you. Leverage the power of good referrals and testimonials. Carefully qualifying referrals and using relevant impact testimonials in a strategic, personalized way will go a long way to shifting those smiles into new business. And what can make you happier than that?

Make the shift

YOU WORK HARD to bring in new customers. It takes effort to hold on to them in the face of fierce competition with no shortage of sharks prepared to drop their prices to "buy" your clients away from you. You can no longer settle for customers. Look for ways to move your princes up the satisfaction scale by making time to understand and consistently deliver on their evolving expectations. Willingly solicit and accept feedback—the good and the constructive. Use these feedback conversations appropriately to encourage clients to provide impact testimonials and qualified referrals.

Above all, recognize that your advocates' words provide the necessary evidence that will help you open new doors within this customer account and provide you with the evidence you need to engage new ones.

Common Nonsense		Uncommon Sense
Satisfy customers	→	Cultivate advocates
The close is the finish line	→	The contract starts the journey
Deliver results	→	Consistently crush expectations
No news is good news	→	Ask: How are we doing? How am I doing?
Sellers are the mouthpiece of their company	→	Be the eyes and ears of your company
Receive smiles	→	Request impact testimonials and qualified referrals
Do it alone	→	Engage your advocates in the sales process

8

DISCIPLINE

Manage

Your Greatest

Sales Asset

Talent without discipline is like an octopus on roller
skates. There's plenty of movement, but you never know if
it's going to be forward, backwards, or sideways.

H. JACKSON BROWN, JR.

I FIRST MET CHRIS when he was new to telephone sales, hungry
to learn and a front-row participant in one of my training
classes. His first question was not about selling. "Jill, is it
OK if I bring food into the classroom?" I assumed that, like
others, he would deposit an unobtrusive apple, banana, or
energy bar on the table in front of him. I was so wrong. It
turned out that in his spare time Chris was a competitive
bodybuilder, and this week he was preparing for competition. Over three days I observed with fascination the hunks
of animal protein that emerged from numerous Tupperware
containers brought into class. And the precision with which
Chris consumed them.

Two years later, when interviewing top sales perform-ers, I reconnected with Chris. He had made his mark within the company. With sales results consistently over target he had become a go-to superstar within his team. I wanted to know what drove his success. "I apply the same discipline to selling as I do to bodybuilding," was his simple answer. "I set goals, identify priorities, and apply a ruthless focus to what's most important. I schedule when, and what, I will do each day and I stick to the schedule. I read and learn from people who are where I aspire to be. My goal is to be a field sales rep in New York City in two years."

Eighteen months later, I interviewed Chris again. And this time I spoke to him over the phone from his new home in New York City.

I see hundreds of enthusiastic salespeople come through training every year, and while many do well, Chris is con-sistently at the top of his field. He is not a member of the "Lucky Sperm Club" of people for whom everything seems to go right. He wasn't born with this talent either. What's his secret? Desire, pigheaded dedication, and the knowledge that nothing happens without *disciplined execution.*

He gets that the greatest asset to his personal success is Chris. Chris manages Chris. He doesn't rely on his manager to drive his sales performance. While others fret over how to get it all done, Chris gets it done. He ruthlessly manages his attention, his mind-set, and his environment. And he continuously reflects on, and learns from, all that he does. He knows that the barrier to any salesperson's success is not lack of time. It's not the size of their market or the pressure of low-cost competition. And it's not the buyer's reluctance to interact. I hate to tell you, but the #1 barrier to your suc-cess may well be you.

The good news is that your greatest asset is also you.

Forget time management

WE ALL HAVE twenty-four hours in a day, seven days in a week, and fifty-two weeks in a year. Nobody gets an extra hour for good behavior. So how is it possible that while many of us have an ever growing to-do list that prevents us from getting the important stuff done, Chris at the next desk has already reeled in 130 percent of his annual quota? With five months of the year still to go!

Who doesn't struggle with this? Juggling existing customers and incoming leads, negotiating with price-conscious buyers, squeezing in new business development activity, attending a multitude of meetings, and keeping up with evolving technologies—all while leaving some "awake time" for family. The consistent question I hear from sales professionals and business owners is, "How do I find a way to manage my time so that I get everything done and keep everyone happy?" Overwhelmed is the new normal. And if you are one of the tribe that believes time management is the answer to getting the important stuff done, think again.

According to neuropsychologist Dr. Paul Pearsall, "Time management is a waste of time." Pearsall refers to attention as the new business currency and warns us that "until we learn to manage our attention, all the self-helpism time management programs in the world will be useless."[1]

> Eliminating overwhelm has nothing
> to do with time management
> and everything to do with how you
> manage your attention.

This is harder to do than to say when we live in a world where myriad online and offline distractions vie for our attention every day, forming unconscious addictions—so much so that we forget we have choice over where we focus that attention. In fact, by getting disciplined with our choices, we will get more done and free up time.

Here's the bottom line. Trying to manage time to get everything done is nonsense. Identify where and when to focus your attention, make the right activity a priority, and you will make the time to get it done.

Reset your GPS

SALES PROS ARE generally good at setting goals. Annual targets come with the territory. Entrepreneurial sellers start each year with a clearly articulated set of objectives. Goals are important; they provide the destination and give your work purpose. However, many people frequently miss the crucial step of determining the most efficient route to that destination. It's critical to identify a handful of things (no more than three to five) that absolutely must happen to get you to your goals. These are your priorities.

Unfortunately, it's become common nonsense to make the ridiculous a priority. Do you start your day opening a daunting list of irrelevant e-mail in your inbox? Does that urgent proposal request from a marginal client encroach on your important business development time? Do you find yourself preparing for every prospect call with equal intensity? Take a close look at what you consciously or unconsciously deem a priority. And if it is a long list, you have to question your definition of the word "priority."

Racing toward the finish line without a disciplined focus on the *handful* of priorities that are integral to accomplishing your goal is like running a marathon with your legs tied together. You may get there, but it is a ridiculously inefficient process.

Replace your lengthy to-do list with two shorter lists that will be invaluable to you in reaching your objectives.

YOUR PRIORITY LIST

Your priority list contains the "must dos": the handful of things you absolutely commit to doing to get to your end goal.

Let's say that my goal is to increase my new business revenue by 20 percent next year. My priority list:

- Identify and connect with more very important prospects.
- Schedule protected blocks of time every week to work solely on new account acquisition.
- Leverage all networks online and offline to obtain qualified warm leads.

These take precedence over everything. Commit your attention to these consistently and regularly. Make them your new habits.

YOUR "STOP-DOING" LIST

I picked up this revolutionary concept from the Jim Collins classic, *Good to Great*.[2] In his words, this practice requires a "remarkable discipline to unplug all sorts of extraneous junk." Translation for sellers: Eliminate the worthless activities that pull your attention away from activities that grow your sales. Multiple studies reveal that sales pros spend too much time and attention on stuff that doesn't drive results. Here are a few examples from my stop-doing list. Yours will be different.

- Stop responding to e-mails at the start of my day.
- Stop trying to multitask. It sucks efficiency out of my day.
- Stop dealing with administrative clutter that others do better than I do.

If you drive to an unfamiliar destination without setting your GPS, you will drive for a long time. And potentially in circles. Sellers need GPS.

G: Goals. Know where you want to go.

P: Priorities. Get there efficiently. And with more sanity.

S: Stop-doing list. Remove the roadblocks and detours that impede your journey.

Still need a reason to switch from time management to attention management? Let me introduce you to Jean-Pierre, a commissioned sales pro whose goal was to drive and maintain revenue that would sustain a healthy six-figure income for him. Getting there required a focus on three priorities:

* Acquire new clients.
* Expand within his existing buying accounts.
* Retain his growth opportunity accounts.

When Jean-Pierre brought on a new high-revenue client, he hit his goal. This one big win shifted his attention. As he became obsessed with protecting his meal ticket from predators, new business acquisition fell off his priority list and retaining this account consumed 100 percent of his focus. A couple of years into the relationship a change of leadership within Jean-Pierre's client company took this cash cow in a direction that no longer required Jean-Pierre's services, and he watched helplessly as his income dropped to a fraction of his previous earnings.

Most of us set goals. But it's common for them to get tucked away in the deepest reaches of our filing system. Even if your clearly defined objectives sit prominently on your home screen, goal setting alone gets you nowhere. Delivering results requires you to commit your attention to the handful of priorities that drive you toward these goals. And the discipline to stop doing what won't.

Schedule and protect

EVAN IS NEW to the company, a firm that provides software, hardware, and managed technology services to businesses of all sizes. He entered the company from a different industry with no customer base or contacts within this business. He does, however, have a sales target. Evan is starting from scratch and he is prospecting for his livelihood.

Evan *schedules* his attention. Do not try to reach him between 7:30 a.m. and 9:30 a.m., because he is on the phone. Every day. "This is the best time to get the right people at their desks. Why would I waste these hours writing or responding to e-mails when it's the optimal time to get a live connection with decision-makers and influencers? That's my #1 priority. Speak to the right people." Every morning Evan has his plan. His call list, color coded according to potential, is on his desk. He has a framework for what he intends to say. All potential distractions are turned off. He is committed.

Most of us schedule our attention to get specific activities done. But scheduling without its better half, protection, is like trying to back up the car without turning on the ignition. Nothing much happens.

Evan fiercely protects his attention for those two hours every morning. When I request an interview for my book at 9:00 a.m., he politely declines and offers me an alternative time of day. Nothing short of the building burning down around him will stop him from getting on the phone to prospect each morning between 7:30 and 9:30. He will not respond to colleagues, he refuses to schedule meetings, he won't let technology intrude. After a few months on the job, Evan has achieved an enviable 50 percent access rate.

Scheduling your attention to work on the important stuff is easy. The hard part is committing to that schedule and protecting it against all distractions. An intriguing e-mail drops into your inbox. A client needs to meet with you. The boss needs an update. A peer drops by your desk to "pick your brain." You plan your day. And then the chaos of your day happens, leaving you with a scant ten minutes of that scheduled hour to develop the creative access campaign that will get you onto the radar of your VIP. Not smart.

Now think about this.

You are in a meeting with your top client, Mr. Bigmoney. He is sharing the specifics of a new initiative that requires the support of a company like yours. As he speaks, do you respond to your e-mail? Of course not. Do you allow colleagues to walk in and out of your meeting? No. Do you stop mid-conversation to work on a marginal lead in your inbox? Duh. And, before this important meeting, if another client requests a meeting at this same time, do you blow off Mr. Bigmoney? You're not crazy. You'd offer another time to that second client. Common sense. Except that it's uncommon to apply it to other priorities in your workday.

Schedule *and protect*. The two go hand in hand. There's a world of difference between planning to do something and getting it done.

Schedule everything, including nothing

ALISON IS A busy sales leader. She is also one of my best clients. She's incredibly smart and committed, and I love any time I can get with her. Over the past four years, as she has taken on an ever-expanding role, I've noticed a pattern. In trying to get everything done, she is failing to get anything done well.

She is a master scheduler. No one gets time with Alison without a formal meeting request with a definitive start and end time. With the rare exception she keeps her meetings to thirty minutes. But with a cast of thousands vying for her time, Alison is harried. She runs her meetings back to back, and I can almost hear her brain trying to catch up with her day. Alison is so caught up in the tempest of busyness that she fails to build in moments of calm. She needs to schedule "between time."

"Between time" provides the opportunity to breathe and to think, both of which are important for people to perform optimally. Scheduling a pause between meetings allows you to reflect on each meeting, to digest nuances of what the client said, and make notes about important insights while they're fresh. You also want to mentally assess the success of your meeting. What went well? What did you miss? Did you get to the client's end goal? And yours? What do you plan to do next? And it's an opportunity to clear your head so that you arrive at your next meeting prepared for a new conversation.

Another productivity booster that has worked for me, and many of my clients, is to schedule my expectations of others. If I've asked you to provide me with something or to get back to me by a certain date, I schedule this commitment in my system. If the date arrives and you haven't delivered, you will hear from me. If you have a reputation for being late with your responses, I'll schedule a reminder to go out a few days before your due date. Knowing your commitment is firmly on my schedule means I can get it off my mind and focus on more important matters.

We live in a world that runs so fast that if we don't schedule something, it won't happen. And that includes the downtime. Get disciplined. Schedule everything. Including nothing.

Bubble wrap your peak performance

MANY OF YOU are too young to remember the 1976 TV movie *The Boy in the Plastic Bubble*, based on a true story of a child born with an improperly functioning immune system. Any contact with other human beings, unfiltered air, or out-side elements of any kind could kill him, and so he lived in incubator-like conditions. Wrapped in a room-sized bubble that ensured nothing got in and that he didn't get out, the boy grew up to be a man.

The only way I was able to complete the most difficult project of my career, this book, by the deadline set by my publisher was to create an impenetrable bubble and spend time in it each day. I got it done by "bubble wrapping" my peak performance hours.

We all have a time of day and set of circumstances when we focus and perform best. Our brain is at its sharpest. Our energy is high. Work seems effortless, and ideas flow. We focus better and work smarter. These are our peak performance hours.

I attack my scariest projects between 7 a.m. and 11 a.m. Like preparing for an important client meeting, creating compelling sales messages for VIPs, writing this book. Mid-afternoon is when my focus wanes, so that's when I schedule tasks that require less thought: e-mail responses, administrative tasks, posting on social media. Or I use that time to re-energize by interacting with others.

If you are looking for a smart way to increase your productivity and accomplish the important projects that sometimes get away from you, start observing your work habits. Notice the time of day when you operate at peak performance.

Create an impenetrable bubble around this time. A physical and mental space where others can't get in and you can't be distracted out. We have so many demands on our attention: keeping up with social media, client follow-up, proposal writing, presentation development, team meetings. Getting the important stuff done without building a protective bubble around it is almost impossible. Commit to *no* distractions.

Notify others that you will not be responding during this time. Turn off all shiny objects and notifications. You heard me. The biggest attention-sucker in today's business world is your inbox. Now I'm not saying you shouldn't deal with e-mail. But I am suggesting you need to rethink how you manage your approach to it. "The average interaction worker spends an estimated 28 percent of the workweek managing e-mail."[3] Every peek at that screen interrupts your peak performance hours and dilutes your ability to focus on what's important.

I studied with brilliant entrepreneur and thought leader Brendon Burchard. His words on this subject are embedded in my brain: "When you start your day by opening your inbox, you immediately put yourself on others' agendas." Think about it. You get to your desk at 8:30 intending to dedicate an hour to new business development. You open your inbox and see a number of e-mails that require a response. The reply isn't needed immediately but, heck, you're here. You might as well get it done. That hour you committed to business growth activities is completely squandered. The one thing you can never get back is time. It's gone. Forever.

We've all read that the most efficient people look at their e-mail a handful of times each day, manage their customers' expectations, and avoid wasting time responding to e-mails that twenty minutes later no longer require their attention. If you're one of those people who say, "Well, that won't work for me," do one of two things: One, get over your big fat ego. Seriously, you're not that important. Or two, find a way that works for you to efficiently manage e-mail.

For example, I prefer not to look at e-mail first thing, as I know it derails my day. But there are many mornings when I have several balls in the air, I am anticipating specific e-mails, and I need to see what's there. I scan my inbox and red flag anything important. But important doesn't necessarily mean urgent. I don't respond immediately. I shut down Outlook and respond to the red flags when I leave my bubble.

On busy days I schedule times in the day to address e-mail. (Remember, schedule everything.) This approach not only improves my productivity immensely, it keeps me sane. Knowing I have time slots allotted to e-mail enables me to focus on the immediate task. A 2014 study from the University of British Columbia found that during a week of "limited e-mail use" (three times per day), participants experienced significantly lower daily stress than during a week of unlimited e-mail use.[4] People actually felt less stressed when they checked their e-mail less often.

Cassy, a member of my virtual marketing team, has an approach that works for her. She manages the expectations of her clients. Her e-mail signature reads as follows: "I check/respond to e-mail at 10:00 a.m. and 2:00 p.m. on weekdays. If you need an immediate, time-sensitive response, please don't hesitate to call or text me." I've never phoned her because I know she will respond at 10:00 and my requests can wait. Her disciplined approach has trained me to work more efficiently.

And if you're still struggling to bubble wrap your peak performance time, give yourself a shake. Are you so addicted to the pull of technology, e-mail, and the attention of others that you've lost sight of what's important? Or are you overvaluing your own self-importance? Will the world really collapse if you disconnect for thirty minutes to work smart?

Three rules for getting it all done

WRITING A BOOK when you run a small business is really really really hard. Yes, three reallys! Even with GPS.

I have a clear goal. To have the book in the market by fall 2017. I know my priorities, the key steps that will get me there:

- Schedule and protect dedicated writing time.
- Research to support my key insights.
- Stick to a tight editorial schedule.

Dedicated writing time is essential to an author. But it is so easy to procrastinate, especially as sitting in front of a computer for great big gobs of time is not a sweet spot for me. I can always find something to distract me from this painful process. And it's no different for you with your own priorities. So how do you set yourself up to stick with them?

RULE #1: KNOW YOUR SPECIFIC NEXT ACTION

Productivity guru David Allen provided me with the antidote to procrastination and indecision with his concept of "next action."[5] Always know your specific next action. When I step to the writing desk on any given day, I know exactly what I plan to get done. The specific chapter. The specific subchapter. The number of words. I have my research files on my desk ready to go. When I sit before the computer I operate at maximum efficiency. I don't dither. Because when I shut down the day before I have already identified my specific next action. I have scheduled it. I have protected it.

For salespeople, specificity of your next action is the miracle cure for procrastination. For best results, always set a realistic action for the allocated timeline. Only got thirty minutes today to work on a big proposal and presentation? Decide on an appropriate next action for that half hour. Maybe it's simply to summarize the key interests of the customer or create a first draft PowerPoint presentation. Maybe draft the executive summary. Make the task fit the time.

RULE #2: STICK TO THE 50 PERCENT PRINCIPLE

Busy salespeople have a tendency to overload their day, overload their client meeting agendas, and overload their sales conversations, all in a valiant attempt to be more productive. But this habit achieves the opposite. There is also a pandemic of naïve optimism that tasks requiring serious and deep thought can be accomplished in short time bursts.

This common nonsense sends our stress levels through the ceiling when we realize we're not going to get the job done, and we're not going to do it well. When we shortchange the tasks that require us to think deeply, like personalizing your company's capabilities presentation for a first meeting with a new VIP, we put the sale in jeopardy.

Brutal truth: Everything worthwhile takes longer than we anticipate. Typically about 50 percent longer. If you think you need forty minutes to write an impactful executive summary for a proposal, schedule a full hour. Otherwise you're racing against the clock, and that causes stress. And when stress levels rise, intelligence drops. Not a good thing when mapping out the one page of your proposal that actually gets read by the decision-maker. And when you bleed over your allocated time, you lose control of the rest of your day.

What's the worst that could happen if you find you don't need that extra 50 percent? You just carved out unanticipated breathing room to prepare for your next meeting, read that important post, or respond to a handful of red-flagged e-mails without detracting from the important priorities. Now that's managing your attention.

RULE #3: ALARM IT

Keeping one eye on the clock pulls at your attention and takes you off focus. Set your alarm for ten minutes before the end time of your scheduled activity. If you've allocated an hour to write that summary, set the alarm for fifty minutes. This allows you ten minutes to complete your final thought, capture your specific next action, and clear your desk.

One hundred percent of your focus will now be on the task at hand because you've delegated the role of timekeeping to your phone. And when you are working for extended periods on larger projects, use your alarm to remind you to take scheduled breaks. Experts suggest working in forty-minute chunks because it is hard to retain focus for longer. Personally, I like to go longer. I prefer to work for sixty minutes and then take a ten-minute break to stretch my legs, get some fresh air, and clear my head.

If you're thinking, "No way can I schedule myself as rigidly as these three rules require," I have three words: *Shift* that thinking. If you want to regain control of your day, get more done at higher quality and with less stress, so that you win better deals in less time, make these three rules of productivity a discipline within your sales practice:

Rule #1: Know your specific next action.
Rule #2: Stick to the 50 percent principle.
Rule #3: Alarm it.

Don't let technology dumb you down

BRIAN, A TECHNOLOGY sales rep, was on the phone speaking to Corey, the IT manager for a new account. It was a brief scheduled call to introduce Brian as the go-to contact for future technology purchases.

While Corey was talking, I noticed Brian skimming his incoming e-mail. He stole a few seconds to fire a short e-mail to a supplier to confirm a different client's order. Brian closed the call by reiterating his enthusiasm to be working with Corey.

Brian and I reviewed the call. While we agreed that this client had no immediate need for Brian's services, it was evident we took two different messages from the same conversation. Corey had briefly mentioned a challenge within his data center, one that suggested a possible future need, and this potential opportunity had blown right by Brian.

Author Nicholas Carr cites a body of work indicating that our attempts to multitask hamper our ability to think deeply and creatively. He cites research that found that heavy multitaskers are "much more easily distracted by 'irrelevant environmental stimuli,'" have "significantly less control over the contents of their working memory," and are generally "much less able to maintain their concentration on a particular task."[6] In short, everything distracts them.

This is bad news for you if you're a salesperson who's trying to do it all, all of the time. In fact, your ability to differentiate yourself through relevance requires you to focus intently on what a customer is saying and to hear the implication of their words. Chances are my rep Brian not only missed an important clue to future opportunity with this new client, he might also have neglected to include an important piece of information in his e-mail to the supplier.

And there's a bigger concern here. Scientists say that the plasticity of our brains means the extensive use of digital media may be having physiological and neurological effects, in essence rewiring our brains to the point where we may become *incapable* of deep thought. Yet the capability for deep thought undoubtedly separates the sales superstars from the average seller. So if you think your reliance on technology is helping you work smarter, think again.

In today's technologically driven, fast-paced, multitasking, mega-surfing world, we are constantly bombarded with distractions and interruptions. I see evidence on every call, in every training class, and on the road, that technology may, in fact, be making us dumber.

And it doesn't simply relate to multitasking.

The robotic use of cookie-cutter scripts, templated presentations, and cut-and-paste proposals certainly helps the seller churn out more with less effort. But your communications to customers do little to position you to be a game changer if they are unaccompanied by the deep thought required to adapt the content and structure to the interests of the specific audience. Similarly, capturing sales rep activity in a CRM system without including the valuable client insights gleaned from the call is a dumb use of an immensely valuable technology.

Our unthinking reliance on technology puts us in danger of creating a sales community of shallow thinkers. And that scares me. Shallow thinking is the archenemy of the game-changing sales pro. It commoditizes both seller and customer. And it's causing super-talented people to fail.

The final nails in the coffin: Twitter, texting, Snapchat, and similar technologies have us communicating in sound bites, to the point where this is now the primary way that some of us absorb information. Just the other day, a local university business student who had scored low on an important assignment held her teacher (a colleague of mine) to task: "I worked hard on this final assignment. It warrants a higher grade."

Her teacher agreed that she had worked hard. They reviewed the written instructions together and quickly discovered that this student's selective reading had caused her to miss an important objective of the assignment. Despite her hard work, her failing grade would stand.

Now imagine the consequences of misinterpreting or missing our customers' words because we skim instead of reading, or we listen selectively. We're doing too much important work inattentively rather than being fully present.

So here are my questions to you:

- What are you doing to manage your use of technology so that you stay focused on your interactions with clients?
- Are you disciplined in scheduling uninterrupted "digitally turned off" think time for important priorities like refining your business development strategy, defining your VIPs, creating thoughtful sales messages, and positioning your proposals to win?

Get off autopilot

I BELONG TO A GYM. I use the term "belong" loosely, as I go there so rarely it is now costing me close to $90 per visit. One time, I was waiting to use the hip abductor machine—a machine that promises the possibility of my 120-pound frame developing thighs that will make Schwarzenegger green with envy. A woman ten years my senior, and a mere five feet to my five-foot-seven amazon frame, finished with the machine and waved me in. I went to move the weight up to my usual one hundred pounds and saw that it was already set to 115 pounds. My ego started to arm-wrestle my brain. I was not about to let a senior citizen pump more weight than me. And so the machine remained at 115 pounds as I completed my normal routine of three times twenty reps. Yes it was harder. My chicken thighs were feeling the burn. But it felt good.

When I moved to the next machine, I took the weight up an extra fifteen pounds. And the next. And the next. At the end of the hour I had completed the best workout in years. I realized I had been short-changing my potential all these years, and robbing myself of a stronger—dare I say hotter—bod. Wasn't that the reason for the gym membership? I was stuck in the rut of habit. It had taken an older, shorter, and evidently fitter woman to kick me out of the comfort of autopilot.

We all shift into autopilot periodically. How many times have you completed the journey to and from work without giving the route a single thought? Or dropped mindlessly onto the couch in front of the TV after a hard day on the job? One place you want to keep your hands firmly on the manual controls is in selling. Avoid the deep muddy rut of habit. If you're using the same "hand me down" approach your boss used fifteen years ago or simply doing what the rest of the industry is doing, it's time to climb out of that rut.

I love Kenichi Ohmae's quote, "Rowing harder doesn't help if the boat is headed in the wrong direction."[7] Trouble is, common nonsense from the helmsman, often the boss, is: Make more calls. Have more meetings. Present more proposals. Translation: Work harder, not smarter. He's putting you on autopilot.

Here is a three-step approach to keep your hands firmly on the controls.

Learn > Act > Reflect

LEARN

Smart sellers know that change is the new status quo. They are constantly refining their craft. They take advantage of a steady flow of accessible education, online and elsewhere, much of it at low or no cost. They read, they subscribe, they follow. They observe other sales and business experts from a range of industries. They are curious about the science of selling, about business, about their clients' markets, and about human behavior.

ACT

I heard a horrific statistic years ago: 75 percent of training workshop attendees, even when motivated to act, fail to apply their newly learned skills. Or, after a very short period of time, they have dropped back into the rut of old habits. To benefit from any learning experience, even this book, choose a handful of insights that will best support your success. Don't try to change everything at once. Commit to executing a newly learned activity every day for thirty days. Share and engage others in your intent—your boss, a buddy, your cheering team—for those times when motivation wanes. Track and share your success. There is no greater motivator for you and your peers than a real-world success story.

REFLECT

Regularly hit the pause button and assess what's working for you—and what's not. Review your results against your activity. When I took the time to reflect on the origins of my new business a few years ago, it was an eye-opening exercise. Over 75 percent of my new clients were a result of networking, a referral, or one of my speaking engagements. In 2010 I committed much of my attention to proactively seeking more referrals and speaking engagements. The result: a 34 percent increase in revenue in a year when many were still struggling in the aftermath of the financial meltdown.

Autopilot is an extremely valuable tool... in ships and airplanes. But if your sales career is on full-time autopilot, it's time to take a step back, flip the switch to manual, and grab hold of those controls.

Stop
creating fiction

A COLLEAGUE GAVE me an important and well-deserved kick in
the pants over lunch. I was griping about my struggle with
the development of a new product, bemoaning all the reasons why I felt it wasn't going to get done.

Her response: "Jill, you need to change your story. This
one isn't serving you." She was referring to the story I had
created in my head as to why this product development process wasn't working for me.

I've been told many times that "the human mind is the
greatest creator of fiction." The stories we create govern our
actions. They can slow us down, or even paralyze us. Or they
can inspire and motivate. Sales professionals are masterful
storytellers. I could compile an entire novel from the fanta-
sies I hear from the field. For example:

- Executives *never* take sales calls.
- Decisions *always* come down to price.
- There's *never* enough time in the day to get the important
  stuff done.
- *Everyone* hides behind voice mail and e-mail.

OK there's some truth to this last one. But we, the selling
community, can take some responsibility for it. As for the
others: utter nonsense. And pure fiction.

Let's take the first example. You've decided to call into
the C-suite. You fire out a handful of e-mail messages to

two executives and you don't hear back. What happens? The gremlin inside your head goes on a rampage with comments like, "Executives don't respond to sellers." Or "I'm not important enough." "I'm useless at this."

All fiction. But pretty soon you start buying into this story. Enough to stop you calling at the executive level.

Now consider the facts:

Fact: You've sent a couple of e-mails to *two* executives.
Fact: Two executives have not responded. Yet!
Fact: Two refusals do not imply the universal truth that every executive will react the same way.

Perhaps one executive is fighting a raging fire elsewhere in his organization. The other was flattened by a bus outside her office just as she was trying to text you a reply. And yes, it is possible that you did call two executives who refuse to deal with salespeople.

The point: You don't know. Don't let these great works of fiction derail you unless you have evidence.

Make decisions based on the facts. Not fiction.

Fiction erodes confidence.
Facts empower you to take action.

Of course you want to take a close look at the messages you send to executives. We've already discussed the common nonsense of attempting to connect with an executive with no evidence of value to someone at her level of the organization. Go back to what you know about this person, company, or market. Leverage other channels to connect. Create your drip campaign. Work the wheel of prospecting. Engage the support of others: the assistant, internal coaches, your own executive. Move on to another prospect and give this one a chance to respond. There are many paths to take when you start with the facts. Fiction leads to a dead end.

Now think about your own inner voice. Do you have a great work of fiction inside your head? If so, follow this four-step process to rewrite your story:

1. Pause.
2. Challenge your thinking. Separate the fiction from the facts.
3. Rewrite your story based on the facts.
4. Then choose the empowering route that will move you forward.

Watch your blind spot

I'M A SUCKER for sports cars. If a car has two doors, sleek lines, and a powerful engine, it calls my name. Years ago I was two weeks into ownership of my turbocharged-anniversary-edition Nissan 350Z and loving my new wheels. Until I made a simple lane change on a Toronto highway. My rearview mirror showed the road behind was open. A glance over my right shoulder confirmed I was clear to move.

Foot on the accelerator I turned the wheel to the right and... My stomach lurched at the jarring blast of someone's horn followed by the acrid smell of rubber tearing on asphalt. Another car was within a millimeter of the new paintwork of my passenger-side door. Its driver flipped me a familiar gesture. He was mad. I was shaken. I did not see it coming.

I found out later from a car buff that, because of its sloped back, the 350Z has a wicked blind spot. Checking the rearview mirror and a quick shoulder-check aren't enough. Unless you twist yourself into a pretzel, it's impossible to see certain points outside the car. I was lucky. The quick reaction of the other driver avoided a day spent in the body shop. Or worse.

Blind spots are equally dangerous in selling.

A blind spot is something you do, or don't do, that is getting in the way of your success. And here's the kicker. You're unaware of it. And if you're not conscious of it, you can't fix it.

I was shadowing Justin on a sales call with a potential new customer. Justin was young, ambitious, and bright.

He was also genuinely interested in business and came to the meeting armed with a handful of smart insights and thought-provoking questions that I knew would engage his customer.

During the call I noticed a disturbing pattern. Justin would ask a question and then immediately, before the customer had a chance to respond, provide an answer. As this behavior repeated itself throughout the call, I realized that Justin was leaving the meeting with his own perspective on this organization's needs. Not the customer's.

When we sat down to debrief the meeting, Justin was ecstatic. He had valuable information that he could now use to move the sales process forward. I hated to burst his happy bubble but I had to ask, "Justin, are you aware that you just had a sales call with yourself?" I shared my observations and followed them with, "Justin, what does the customer need to do when confronted with your big questions?"

"I guess he needs to think."

"And what happens when people are thinking?"

"They are silent."

Bingo! Justin realized that his discomfort with silence, coupled with an empathetic desire to help a customer find answers, was a self-defeating trait.

Blind spot eliminated.

A blind spot can also be a lack of awareness of one of your strengths. Alan was thrown into training within months of starting his field sales career. On the last day of training he was required to role-play, on camera, following several considerably more seasoned colleagues. Serious pressure. He had fifteen minutes to present his company's capabilities to a fictitious executive, played by yours truly, and a middle manager played by Connelly, a member of Alan's leadership team.

At the end of the presentation, Connelly and I gaped at each other, jaws on laps. "Sold!" we said in unison. I turned to Alan. "Are you aware of how masterfully you positioned your company's capabilities against our priorities?" He wasn't. We had uncovered a blind spot.

With additional feedback from his peers, we walked him through his presentation step by step, shining a light on specific behaviors and their impact on the two distinct levels of buyer he was presenting to. This newbie's confidence soared. More importantly, this newfound awareness puts him in a position to ruthlessly leverage these strengths to outperform more experienced sellers in the real world. Imagine if he had continued in his new career blind to one of his greatest personal talents and differentiators.

Blind spots are common. Even the most experienced of us has blind spots. Particularly as the business environment continues to evolve, our experience itself can create blinkered vision. The mother of all blind spots is highlighted by the statistic I shared in chapter 1: that over half of sellers are operating under the assumption that their sales approach helps them stand out from their competitors. Yet, in the eyes of their customers, it doesn't.

So how do we get out of the dark?

It goes back to proactively and regularly soliciting feedback on your sales approach at every opportunity and from multiple sources: your manager, peers, trainers, and customers. Do not be tempted to discount or defend. Listen from a place of curiosity. Accept their input graciously. Thank each person for their support. Then decide if and how you want to act on the feedback.

Rethink your paralyzing questions

MOST SALESPEOPLE I KNOW would happily trade their next fat bonus check to get answers to their biggest, most troublesome questions. I hear these big hairy sales questions in the training room and at the end of conference presentations, and I see them on numerous LinkedIn groups, as sellers seek counsel from anyone willing to unload their "expert" advice to those willing to listen.

Here are a few recent examples:

1. How do I show this client that I'm different from the other salespeople?
2. How many times can I follow up with a prospect before it becomes irritating?
3. How do I justify our higher rate?

In these examples the question itself is common nonsense. Asking yourself questions about your sales approach is generally a good thing, but questions like these are paralyzing rather than productive. They are coming from a place that's counterproductive; they start with negative assumptions that create the kind of self-talk that inhibits your ability to move to a productive solution.

The first step in getting answers to these perennial conundrums is to reframe the question to enable action. Come at these big hairy challenges with a different mind-set.

I've been asked by potential new clients to come to a first meeting prepared to answer, "How is salesSHIFT different from sales training companies X and Y?" But that's not a productive way to frame the question—not for the seller, and not for the buyer. Isn't the better question to pose to yourself and then answer for the client: "How is salesSHIFT more relevant to this stakeholder and her company's current objective?"

There is no definitive answer to question #2, "How many times can I follow up with a prospect before it becomes irritating?" The uncommon sense answer is: "It depends." I've seen laughable responses posted online, but none of that helps move you forward.

Here's the more constructive reframe: "Given what I know about this prospect, the urgency of their interest, and the relevance of my offering, what makes sense in terms of frequency and content from the buyer's point of view?"

The third question, "How do I justify our higher rate?" has many sellers spinning their wheels.

Reframe: "How do I use what I know about my customers to position our services so that the rate is viewed as fair value?"

A second reframe to this one: "How do I proactively connect with potential customers that value the specific services we offer at our fair rate?"

The problem with your big hairy sales questions isn't the lack of an answer. The problem is how you pose the question itself. Reframing the question focuses you on the problem differently and opens up the possibility of fresh thinking that enables, rather than disables, productive action on your part.

Do you also notice how each of the original three questions is seller focused? And the reframed questions focus on the customer? Hmm.

Sometimes our heads are our biggest roadblock. Here's a fun assignment. Think of a sales challenge. Write down the related question that you've been struggling to answer. Share the question with your colleagues. Is your question enabling or disabling? Seller or customer focused? Have each team member reframe the question and then select and commit to answering the smarter question. That question will shift your thinking and help move you forward.

Make the shift

THERE IS NO OTHER way to say this. Discipline is the bedrock of sales success.

High performers are relentless in how they prioritize and manage their attention. They are disciplined in their thinking, dedicating appropriate time and energy to the elements of their job that require uninterrupted quality focus.

Not afraid to say no to traditional distractions, they are fiercely protective of the time committed to the priorities they know will accelerate achievement of their goals.

These superstars take direct responsibility for their personal and professional growth. And they never lay blame at the feet of the client, the boss, or the market conditions. They've found their mojo because they choose to manage their greatest sales asset. Themselves.

Common Nonsense	→	Uncommon Sense
Manage time	→	Prioritize attention
Set goals	→	Reset your GPS: Goals. Priorities. Stop-doing list.
Schedule	→	Schedule and protect
The lure of distraction	→	Bubble wrap your peak performance time
Autopilot	→	Learn. Act. Reflect
Fiction derails your success	→	Facts empower you
Blind spot	→	Self-awareness
Ask questions that paralyze your thinking	→	Reframe your questions to enable answers

CONCLUSION

Make It Matter

I SAID IT AT THE OUTSET. Selling is common sense. Deep down inside, you already know this, and what you've read is a much-needed reminder, a shot in the arm, or validation that you're in the enviable 25 percent that consistently stands out in the eyes of your customers. We all "get it." Intellectually.

But there's one colossal problem: the assumption that knowing is doing.

Of course you know this stuff. But knowing isn't doing. Whether you sell radio advertising to Mr. and Mrs. Jones's Emporium down the street, or multimillion dollar IT service agreements to global enterprises, or anything in between, the important question that requires your candid answer is this: "How consistently do I apply the uncommon sense of selling smarter?"

Sometimes I feel that we have lost sight of who we are and why we sell. Last time I looked we are still human beings influencing other human beings. Sales skills are fundamental business and communication skills. The foundation of good selling lies in the intent to be of service to the customer. To *contribute* to their success. Sadly, these fundamentals are often replaced by techniques or tactics that consciously or unconsciously manipulate the decisions of others for our own gain—the common nonsense that has made "sell" a four-letter word and leaves many sales professionals questioning a role that is the lifeblood of business growth.

It's time to make the shift. Ditch the common nonsense and master the new ABCs of selling. Reset your perspective to be focused on the customer. Commit to the right input to achieve the highest output. Above all, never lose sight of the fact that every interaction with your prospects and customers is a once-in-a-lifetime moment of truth. Give these moments the respect and deep thought they warrant.

You've just invested several hours of your life reading this book. That's a significant investment of time in a busy world. So make it count. Hit the pause button. Step into your customer's shoes. Decide now what you will do differently to be relevant in the eyes of the people who matter—your existing and future customers. Commit to the uncommon sense that will make you stand out from your competitors, win more business at higher prices, and create lifelong advocates. Make this moment of truth matter to your sales success.

Good selling!

The Frameworks at a Glance

Focus on the right input. Rewrite your selling ABCS. *(Chapter 1)*

Always Be Contributing
Always Be Curious
Always Be Connecting

Your ticket to access is evidence. Know what is TOP of mind to your prospect. *(Chapter 2)*

T: Trends and Threats
O: Objectives and Opportunities
P: Priorities and Problems

Position your sales messages, presentations, proposals, and conversations to stand out. *(Chapters 2 and 5)*

L: Lead with the customer's interests
C: Connect your value
B: Be specific
S: Say less with more impact

Change the rules of the game. Explore all four quadrants of discovery. *(Chapter 4)*

Q1: The business
Q2: The opportunity
Q3: The buying situation
Q4: The stakeholders

Ask fewer, smarter questions to serve both you and the buyer. *(Chapter 4)*

EiQ: Educated insight + Question

Put the customer at the heart of your positioning statement. Give your words a little CPR. *(Chapter 5)*

C: The Customers for whom you do your best work
P: The Priority or Problem you address
R: The Results you achieve

Turn an immediate No into a future Yes. EARN the right to move forward. *(Chapter 6)*

E: Demonstrate Empathy for the customer's situation
A: Ask an open-ended "opinion" question that engages
R: Retreat, leaving the customer wanting more
N: Gain commitment to a Next step

Deliver faster results. Reset your GPS. *(Chapter 8)*

G: Goals. Know where you want to go
P: Priorities. Identify a handful of priorities to get there
    efficiently and with more sanity
S: Stop-doing list. Remove the roadblocks and detours that
    impede your journey

Continue
the Journey

THANK YOU FOR reading this book. For making it to the very last page.

Sales is a big topic, and this is a small book. It is impossible to cover everything and to include all of the "what ifs" that surface along the sales journey. If you liked what you read, but you need more of the "how to," you'll want to hook into these salesSHIFT resources:

- Invite me to inspire your team at your next company or association conference.
- Bring our interactive sales skills development labs or training programs to your company.
- Access our small-team mentoring and coaching process.

Visit our website www.salesSHIFT.ca to join the salesSHIFT community and take advantage of a number of free resources to keep you on track:

- Your weekly Monday Motivation: thirty-second sales tips delivered directly to your inbox at the start of every sales week.
- The salesSHIFT two-minute video series: short video tips that answer your pressing sales questions.
- "Take the Pain out of Prospecting": the audio download you can listen to while on the go.

- The "Uncommon Sense Coaching Guide": simple steps to using this book as an ongoing developmental tool in your sales meetings so that you achieve results.

I wrote this book because I want sales professionals like you to achieve the success to which you aspire. So I want to hear from you. Fire me an e-mail, tweet a message, or invite me to connect on LinkedIn (just don't use the generic invitation!)—let me know how you fare.

Acknowledgments

DECIDING TO WRITE a book is easy. It starts with a vision and the desire to get an important message into the world. Writing the book is like tackling a mammoth. You don't realize just how big it is until you stand before it.

A cast of thousands has contributed over the years to the output of this book and I want to acknowledge a handful by name.

To my husband, John, who for the past year has shared a home with his perfectionist wife and her pet mammoth—a frightening combination. Thank you for your unending patience.

There aren't enough words to express my gratitude to Lynne Morinan, my talented graphic designer, for her extraordinary ability to turn my indecipherable sketches into masterful images. And to Anne Turnbull, Morag Donald, and Lynn Hidy, who selflessly volunteered time from their busy lives to read my rough manuscript and contribute their invaluable feedback.

Thank you to Mike, of the Michael Snell Literary Agency, who guided me through the difficult first steps of the book-writing journey. And, of course, the collaborative team at Figure 1 publishing. Jennifer Smith, Karen Milner, Jessica Sullivan, Diana Byron, Eva van Emden, Renate Preuss, and everyone behind the scenes, thank you for supporting my vision, accepting my quirks, and creating the tangible output of my life's work.

I am forever grateful to my clients and colleagues whose stories, feedback, and inspiration have helped me to build my business and now, my latest victory, tame this mammoth.

And finally to the person who has taught me that, with faith, you can accomplish anything at any stage in life. Thank you to my insanely smart and courageous mum, Dorie.

Notes

Chapter 1

1 Phil Kreindler and Gopal RajGuru. "What Really Matters in B2B Selling." Infoteam in cooperation with the *Harvard Business Manager*, 2014.

Chapter 2

1 Phil Kreindler and Gopal RajGuru. "What Really Matters in B2B Selling." Infoteam in cooperation with the *Harvard Business Manager*, 2014.
2 Mary Shea. "The B2B Sales Force Digital Reboot." Forrester research, October 2015.
3 Phil Kreindler and Gopal RajGuru. "What Really Matters in B2B Selling." Infoteam in cooperation with the *Harvard Business Manager*, 2014.

Chapter 3

1 David Newman training. See also: David Newman. *Do It! Marketing.* AMACOM, 2013.
2 Sara Radicati and Justin Levenstein. "E-mail statistics report." The Radicati Group Inc., 2013–2017.
3 Trish Bertuzzi. *Inside Sales Experts Blog.* The Bridge Group Inc., February 2011. www.bridgegroupinc.com.
4 Jamie Shanks. *Social Selling Mastery.* John Wiley and Sons Inc., 2016.

Chapter 4

1 Phil Kreindler and Gopal RajGuru. "What Really Matters in B2B Selling." Infoteam in cooperation with the *Harvard Business Manager*, 2014.
2 David Schwartz. *The Magic of Thinking Big.* Simon & Schuster, 1987.
3 "Sales Performance Optimization Study: 2016 Win More Analysis." CSO Insights, a business division of Miller Heiman Group, Inc., 2016.

Chapter 5

1 Simon Sinek. *Start with Why*. Penguin Group, 2009.
2 Hubspot Sales Perception Survey Q1 2016.
3 Phil Kreindler and Gopal RajGuru. "What Really Matters in B2B Selling." Infoteam in cooperation with the *Harvard Business Manager*, 2014.

Chapter 6

1 Phil Kreindler and Gopal RajGuru. "What Really Matters in B2B Selling." Infoteam in cooperation with the *Harvard Business Manager*, 2014.

Chapter 7

1 "Sales Performance Optimization Study 2016." CSO Insights, a business division of Miller Heiman Group, Inc., 2016.
2 Hubspot Sales Perception Survey Q1 2016.

Chapter 8

1 Paul Pearsall. *The Last Self-Help Book You'll Ever Need*. Basic Books, 2005.
2 Jim Collins. *Good to Great*. HarperBusiness, 2001.
3 Michael Chui, James Manyika, Jacques Bughin, Richard Dobbs, Charles Roxburgh, Hugo Sarrazin, Geoffrey Sands, and Magdalena Westergren. "The Social Economy: Unlocking Value and Productivity through Social Technologies." McKinsey Global Institute, 2012.
4 Kostadin Kushlev and Elizabeth W. Dunn. "Checking email less frequently reduces stress." *Computers in Human Behavior* 43 (February 2015) pp. 220–228.
5 David Allen. *Getting Things Done*. Penguin Books, 2002.
6 Nicholas Carr. *The Shallows: What the Internet Is Doing to Our Brains*. W.W. Norton and Company Inc., 2011.
7 Kenichi Ohmae, organizational theorist, management consultant.

Index

NOBODY NEEDS
YOUR INFORMATION

YOUR UVP IS VALUELESS

Persistence is irritating

STOP KISSING FROGS

BEING THE BEST IS OVERRATED

Ask the
tough questions

NOBODY NEEDS YOUR INFORMATION
IRRITATING STOP KISSING FROGS BEIN
SO MANY QUESTIONS PRICE IS A COF
DON'T WANT CUSTOMERS ASK THE TO
BUYERS ARE IMPERFECT STOP CREAT
DUMB YOU DOWN FORGET TIME MANA
HAVE THE COURAGE TO SAY NO YOUR E
YOUR INFORMATION YOUR UVP IS V
STOP KISSING FROGS BEING THE B
MANY QUESTIONS PRICE IS A COP-
DON'T WANT CUSTOMERS ASK THE TO
BUYERS ARE IMPERFECT STOP CREAT
DUMB YOU DOWN FORGET TIME MANA
HAVE THE COURAGE TO SAY NO YOUR E
YOUR INFORMATION YOUR UVP IS V
STOP KISSING FROGS BEING THE BEST
QUESTIONS PRICE IS A COP-OUT FO
WANT CUSTOMERS ASK THE TOUGH QU
ARE IMPERFECT FORGET TIME MANAG